For the Record

a documented narrative by Janice Covel

Library of Congress Control Number 2011916555

Manhattan Publishing Company, Sacramento, California
United States of America

First Edition

ISBN 978-0-9614454-3-0

Dedication

Thank you! My heartfelt thanks to all of you who have helped me gather facts, remembrances of times gone by, suppositions about the politics and life styles of those 19th and 20th century days, and your passionate responses about life in Galesburg and Riverside. Dozens and dozens of you helped me bring Eugenia/Eugenie Fuller to the present in the real sense of her dedication to inspiring others to be the best they could be and to believe that learning is a joy forever.

All of you have helped preserve memories of this educator whose personal writings were lost. Her influence has prevailed, and I am thankful to be able to introduce her to others and keep my promise. Teachers have remarkable influence on the course of history as their dedicated students carry on the legacies of their mentors, and they in turn become mentors to others. Because you are reading this, Eugenie Fuller's inspirational legacy lives on.

My gratitude extends to librarians, courthouse employees, cemetery officials, and newspaper archives' workers in both Galesburg and Riverside who have made authenticity a goal with me **for the record.** Thank you all.

Eugenia Fuller

Eugenie Fuller

Prologue

An Assignment
1933

Janice could hardly wait to tell her mother about her early morning dream. She knew it was early morning because she had awakened when her brother closed the front door to go to work, and it was still dark outside. The dream came after that and was such a glorious and strange one that she awakened with a strong determination to make it come true.

"Mom, Mom, where are you?"

"I'm in the kitchen. Where are you?" They laughed and hugged as they met.

"You're all fired up already."

"Yes, 'cause of a dream I had. A lady came to visit me, and she stood close by and smiled at me. I could tell she liked me, and Mom, she was so pretty. She had reddish hair and it was pulled back, like this," and Janice pulled her hair back to show how it was. "Mom, she had the most sparkling green eyes – just like mine – you say I'm always asking questions and getting into mischief, and you say that you can tell by my eyes. Well, her eyes were just like that, and she had dimples. Like mine, only deeper."

"Goodness, that sounds more like a vision than a dream, but then did she talk to you?"

"Yes, and her voice was low, and it was one that you couldn't argue with – like yours. She said, "You are the one to tell our stories. Yes, one day, you will tell our stories.""

"What stories? And what did you say?"

"Say? I didn't say a word. I didn't know what she was talking about. But I remember every word she said. She said, "You will have a curious life – it will have great joys, but it will not be easy. That's why you must write the stories. Mine have mistakenly been destroyed and yours must still be written. I will help you.""

"Then she was gone. Just like that. But you know something? I could hear a swish, swish after she was gone."

"Do you remember what she wore? That's always a good way to date a dream – to tell if the person in the dream is in our time or in the past."

"Yes, she had on a long skirt and a blouse that was decorated with embroidery – the kind you do – and the top of the blouse was up to her neck."

"So what do you think the dream meant?"

"That I must be a good girl, learn a lot, and some day write stories."

"Well, you can write about your life, but you will have to guess about hers unless you find out who she was and then study and study about her life. Do you think you would recognize her picture if you saw it?"

"Oh, yes, Mom. You know what I remember most? The expression on her face. And she will help me. She gave me her word."

"Well, before I fix your eggs, you better sit down and write what you remember. Otherwise, passing time will make you forget." Mom handed Janice a yellow tablet and a pencil. "What will you call your dream friend?"

"Ummm. Your name is Myrta. I can't call her that. I will name her Myra. Mom, do you think I'm silly?"

"No, Janice, not at all. Years ago, I, too, had a dream like yours. I thought I would remember all the details. Time passed. I should have written it down."

Janice turned to a clean page in the tablet. "What is today, Mom?"

"May 28, 1933."

Soon, hot cocoa was on the table, the biscuits came out of the oven, and the eggs sizzled in the skillet. Janice had finished writing.

Janice handed the papers to her mom, and said, "They're not neat at all." Her mother nodded and smiled just a bit. "Your phonetic spelling is very good, and it's readable. Be sure to put these pages with your treasures. Someday, they might be important to you. Now let's eat this breakfast while it's hot."

I didn't realize it at the time, but in retrospect, I know that this was the start of my promised proclivity to write stories as the beautiful lady in the dream had asked me to do.

Preface

Why spend nearly half of my life studying, researching, and living the life of Eugenia (ie) Fuller? How can one person from a far removed generation, a vast geographical distance, and unrelated in any way have such a profound influence on another's life? The second question answers the first, and that's why, at long last, I must share it with you.

I found Eugenie Fuller's name listed as an early and influential educator in Riverside, California as I did research for my dissertation at the University of California, Riverside. My study focused on career patterns of educators in Riverside County from 1870-71 to 1974-75 to determine which paths led to administrative careers, how and when those careers peaked, the reasons for demotions or releases, and the importance of sponsorship.

Subsequent interviews with senior citizens who remembered Miss Fuller with clarity and preciseness revealed a remarkable profile of a school administrator as the principalship was becoming institutionalized as an integral part of school organization. To emphasize the unusualness of the career pattern, it is useful to point out that Miss Fuller was the only female secondary principal in the history of Riverside County for more than 105 years. At the time she was principal, she was the highest paid administrator in the county. She was on a first name basis with the leaders of both Berkeley and Stanford Universities, and her detailed recommendations opened admission doors for many of her students.

1886-1933 is the Riverside emphasis in the manuscript you are about to read, but to really understand Miss Fuller, I knew that I had to find out, too, about her life before she came to "Paradise on Earth." That would take me to Galesburg, Illinois and its outlying communities, and back in time to the mid-1800s.

That was an early settlement period, similar to the formation of the Riverside colony in California more than a quarter century later. Both communities were planned, and both were settled by people determined to emphasize the importance of education, moral values, and propriety. Citizens bought into the plan, the fertile soil, and the expected lifestyles with a strong commitment. They were not pioneers in the sense of running away from problems, searching for the pot of gold, or living a renegade lifestyle.

There is a dearth of information about the Samuel Fuller family in the North Henderson settlement just east of Galesburg, and after many years of seeking facts, I've had to rely on hearsay, interviews, courthouse records, genealogical records, newspapers, school district records, testimonials, writings of others, and intuition to give you, the reader, a sense of her early life. Some points of view of the anecdotes are delineated in third person for background purposes; others are in her own words, some intuitively inspired, and some used from quotes of others. The Riverside years are based on historical and school district records, handwriting analysis, newspaper articles, contemplative assumptions, speeches of public record, and interviews of her students, friends, associates, and critics. I hope you enjoy her journey and find that recognizing the influence one teacher can make will have a lasting impression on your life, too.

Table of Contents

Another Leg of the Journey
Circa 1850

Samuel's shoulders drooped as he looked about his abode. Quickly closing the door, he beheld his wife sleeping in the high-backed rocker with baby Charlotte in her arms. Lucinda's face was tear-stained and her normally coiffed hair was a dark tumble about her smudged face. Only this morning, she had backed away from him because she was so ashamed that her only dress was stained with curdled milk and reeked of grease that had soaked her skirt when the can she was filling fell off the table and onto the floor.

Embers still glowed in the fireplace dyed with soot and smoke, but the barren room was cold, the wood bin had only starting chips, and the day was darkening. Dismal. Dismal. It was time to move on. Time to move to a place with loamy soil instead of glaciated rock with only pockets that could be tilled. Time to move away from mosquitoes spawning in the marshland, rattlesnakes and copperheads roaming the woods surrounding their cabin, and several neighbors who were so suspicious of others that their pointed rifles were part of attempted conversations.

Lucinda stirred. Her eyes opened to Samuel's gaze, and the look on his face told her that her persistent and determined man was ready to move on – again. She was more than ready. They had talked about heading to the Log City – Galesburg community. There, so they'd heard, good level farm land was all around – and for a good price, some said a dollar twenty-five an acre. The best part was the people. It was a fact that men of principle, morality, and charity had been gathering for a few years so they could honor God by educating the brain. They'd even built a college. Lucinda's older brother was already there, and he'd sent word that it was close to Eden. It was either that, Samuel thought, or they'd head back east to a life that he'd tried so hard to escape. At least, they had food and clothes and a doctor, and the loneliness there was not destroying the soul, as here. He broke the silence by asking, "What are we to do?"

As if on cue, lightning struck nearby with a bright zap, and then a loud clap of thunder vibrated the cabin. Within moments, rain fell in torrents. All chance of finding dry wood for the fireplace that night would be for naught. What to do, indeed.

A few weeks later, Samuel and Lucinda Fuller had sold their stake and loaded their treasures – the high-backed rocker, the sea worthy trunk, two framed family pictures, a painting once owned by Lucinda's parents, an oval mirror wrapped in layers of rags, Samuel's old family Bible, a little brown teapot, and stained letters – letters from kin and friends that they were unlikely to see again. Then they added household items that would fit. The rest would be left behind.

On a clear, sunny morning, they held each other and prayed for the future, mounted the wagon, cradled baby Charlotte in a clean blanket that Lucinda had washed in cold water and dried in the mid-day sun the day before, and signaled the team of horses to head west.

They didn't glance back.

Home

Along the way, Samuel Fuller and Lucinda Koontz Fuller met others who were traveling towards Galesburg, the purported Garden of Eden community that had been advertised in pamphlets and by word of mouth by Reverend George Washington Gale and his followers as a sanctuary for those who loved the Lord, cherished education, and lauded manual labor. All three values were to be incorporated in Prairie College (later, Knox), the highest building priority in establishing the town as a place of worth. Reverend Gale's final selection for his settlement in 1836 was a large section of fertile land and level topography midway between the Illinois and Mississippi Rivers in western Illinois as a place to farm and do business, build a college, and preach the word of God – in his Presbyterian belief. The community had been carefully planned and platted with firm investment commitments of money and artisanship, ensuring success for a village they would build in the middle of nowhere, one hundred sixty miles west of Chicago. Galesburg – often called "paper city" because of the careful paper planning – was originally designed to be six blocks in each direction, but allowance had to be made for a creek that ran though the proposed town. There were to be forty-two blocks in all. It was said that the layout was so precise that the map of Galesburg could be drawn by using only a ruler.

"The founders of the city were all of one kind, typical Yankees with several New England generations behind them; of English origin. They were alike in birth, education, religion and means. All they had was their land. The few hired men brought from the East were socially equals and ate at the same table." (Calkins, p. 19)

Outsiders, like Samuel and Lucinda, were drawn there for the security of a tight community, even though they would live somewhere on the outskirts of the village. The three-pronged belief system was another drawing factor: religion, opposition to slavery, and opposition to alcohol (although the word got out that bootlegging flourished).

The area was not unexplored territory. Hoosiers – people from Indiana – had settled mainly in southern Illinois, and some lived just south of the newly planned community. Galesburgers looked down on them as did much of the general population in northern Illinois because the Hoosiers were reputed to be brash people, sloppy housekeepers, and not at all like the Yankees. Other groups were mentioned in the review of the literature, but always as outsiders or disparaged settlers. Indians were mentioned scarcely at all, and hostilities appeared to be absent, yet the natives had been part of the land for centuries and were certainly displaced by the new arrivals.

The Fullers and two traveling families converged at a likely campsite one evening and formed lifelong friendships in a matter of hours. The travelers had left Reverend Gale's community in New York months ago and wearily confided that they were way behind some of their neighbors because of their reluctant, heartrending separations from family members whom they might never see again. That opened the door for everyone to discuss how difficult it was to leave relatives and friends behind. And how difficult it was to give up treasured belongings that would not fit into the wagons or trunks or survive a long trip by land or water. Some sailing vessels went to New Orleans and then on up the Mississippi to Oquawka, the closest point to the new settlement. Once there, the treasures had to set out in the unpredictable weather until wagoners could make the trip to pick them up and take them to the Log City settlement where the pioneers "camped" until their homesteads were completely ready for habitation in Galesburg.

Many pioneers in the 1800s chose to make the long and difficult treks across the states and territories to fulfill a need for adventure. The spirit had to be powerful to even contemplate such a journey. For those escaping criminal justice, the choice of hieing west was far easier than facing punishment in their local stomping grounds. Others, like Samuel and

Lucinda and their new friends, yearned for a homestead in a community where they could build a life together. They were young, curious, and adventurous. 'We can do anything and succeed' was a mantra spoken under their breath, and acted out confidently – at least in the so-called last legs of their journey and on warm spring days with ebullient white clouds moving in the same direction. Even so, it is hard to imagine how the women coped with young children and infants who required constant and tender care, with intense anxiety when the children became ill, and with the deep mourning when deaths occurred and the burials were made along the wayside.

Not only did established residents in the East head westward in the mid-1800s, immigrants from Europe reached the shores and kept on going toward the prairies. It's been said that the primitive roadways were white with covered wagons – and all these pioneers made the journey even though they had little or no hope of ever again seeing loved ones they left behind after tearful goodbyes and remonstrations. The more prosperous people could afford to travel by steamboat and could cover the distance in about two weeks. Trains wouldn't be a common mode of transportation for years. For all, the West's beckoning was an inexorable pull and letters from enticers in Illinois and other frontiers gave them the extra determination to take a fork in life's road.

Those aiming to reach Log City, a rustic cabin community that pioneers built and lived in before they could reside in Galesburg where temporary housing was forbidden, hoped for some of the cabins to be vacated and available to be used by newcomers. For the few fortunate ones, it was a great relief to be welcomed with food, shelter, and emotional sustenance for embarking on entirely different lifestyles. In ensuing weeks, newcomers scanned the countryside and chose options they could afford with eyes on future ownership once they were established.

Samuel and Lucinda spent their last dollars on some acreage in the North Henderson area, a countryside north of Galesburg without ties to the expectations of Galesburgers, but in sympathy and mostly agreeing with their philosophies.

First came a makeshift cabin, then working for other farmers, then plowing and sowing and harvesting on their own homestead, and later adding more land, having a house raising, planting an orchard of fruit trees and finally investing in fine horses and cattle, Samuel's long time dream. Nightmarish memories faded. Life was good and chapters in their lives enhanced the American dream. Charlotte was joined by Emily – both named for the Bronte sisters – and a bit later, plans were made for another baby in the house.

Headed toward the Fuller Homestead

Princess Eugenia
1857

Light, feathery snow blanketed the ground – but barely – leaving tips of gravel and sprigs of grass wet and exposed. Clouds hanging heavy and low were infrequently pierced with shafts of sunlight that appeared suddenly and disappeared just as quickly, leaving an air that was chill and a hush that someone described like closing a door after having said goodbye to a dear friend. It was a strange kind of day. Ominous.

Dr. Moulton cursed the mud and steepness of Fuller Hill as his horses slid from their grips and tried to steady themselves long enough to take another step forward. He cursed himself a little for not remembering the ground was soft, that the thaw from the harsh winter was still in progress and was barely masked by the unusual snowfall. Had he remembered, he chided himself, he could have left the horses and buggy at the foot of the hill by the creek bed and made right more time trudging up over the meadow, through the trees and the newly cleared cemetery lot to the farmhouse. As it was, he was better off to struggle to the top of Fuller Hill than to try to back down the winding, steep stretch filled with treacherous drops that could sink an axle.

His only mental relief was that the message brought to him earlier in the day indicated Mrs. Fuller was thought to be in good health, the baby in normal position, and that he was not the family's only medical hope – not that he approved of the neighborhood midwife. He mused that she was probably really a witch – she certainly acted like she had strange powers. The crazy woman had delivered dozens of babies in the county round about, and the only ones she'd lost were the three or four who had been born deformed. The thought stuck in his head that their deaths were not

7

accidents – that she had cast a spell. There was never a mark to show cause for the deaths.

Miss Orphie had attended the birthings and each time, before any questions could be asked, had said earnestly as a minister would intone to a congregation – "The family had a blessing and it has already gone to be with the Lord. Praised be the Lord."

But it was a strange coincidence when the Goins family out the road apiece had this child with the big head, and it lived – existed – for more than two years. Mrs. Goins was heard to murmur many times – 'if only Miss Orphie had been here when little Frederick was born...'

Just a few more slips and slides and the breathless, glistening horses would be on near level ground – then just a few more wheel turns and on into the drive and up to the tethering pole. Tall, overalled Mr. Fuller greeted him and edged the horses into the yard as he signaled some farmhands to quickly attend the grooming and caring needs. The familiar half circle made by his raised arm was more of an alert than the call of "Men, help is needed!"

"Welcome, Doc. You have my thanks for getting here. Come on in." John Moulton and Sam Fuller shook hands. The two men walked the short distance to the house in a matter of seconds and had no time to offer more than the barest civilities to each other.

"Sam," Dr. Moulton said as they reached the door, "this time I hope you get the son you've long wanted."

"No matter, Doctor. What God wills, I will be grateful for. Lucinda and our little Charlotte and Emily bless and fill my heart, and there's still room for a daughter or a son. No matter, really."

The chimes of the treasured floor clock struck three as they entered the kitchen. The doctor turned to the pan of hot water on the pantry board, dipped his hands, and wiped them with the cloths provided on the table. He paternally patted the shoulders of Charlotte and Emily who were standing silently nearby in the front room and moved quickly to the bedroom in time to be greeted by strong, restrained groans, an explicit sigh, and the cry of a new born. Yes, Miz Orphie was in charge. Dr. Moulton reappeared in the front room a few minutes later with the announcement, "You have a daughter, Sam – a tiny princess."

"A princess, you say. Strange you should say that. The Missus has been reading about Princess Eugenia and has had her heart set on the name of Eugenia should we be blessed with a daughter. So be it. Charlotte and Emily, my loves, what will your father do with three lovely princesses until your Napoleons come riding by?"

"Oh, Papa," Charlotte laughed as she threw her arms around her father's neck and Emily grabbed onto his legs. "Oh, Papa, we want always to stay with you. Will you permit us to see Eugenia and Mama now?"

Miss Orphie joined the group and later walked outside with the good doctor. "Like manna from heaven, this snow is, and soon it will melt and come to naught except as the water soaks in and brings strength to the young growing plants. And so will be the effects of this new life. Look at the heavy sky with only fleeting moments of sunshine. It is a portent of her life."

"Now Miss Orphie. Begone with your tales. You foretell futures and cast spirits and cause our tongues to waggle. Where will your talents lead you? It's dangerous talk."

"Doctor – your hands. I saw you deftly perform surgery last week. You found the bullet in Nazareth Brown's shoulder and cut it out. What gives you the talent?"

"A special sensitivity, Miss Orphie. That's what I call it and a special Power almost projects my hands and guides my judgment."

"And that, my good doctor, is the same sensitivity and Power which helps me speak the truth about what is going to be. We are blessed, Doctor, you and I. And may you grow to respect my talents as I do yours. Good day, Sir." She swirled her skirt about her to keep it from dragging in the mud, slightly curtsied and turned toward home. He watched her a few moments as she stepped carefully, then firmly, and then walked quickly, with straightened posture, before he turned back to the front room. In the open family Bible laid out on the library table, he entered, as was his wont,

Eugenia Fuller, borne 25 May 1857. A few minutes past the hour of 3:00. In the afternoon. All vital signs healthy. A small brown mark on the left side of the neck. May God grant strength and courage to this tender soul.   *Dr. J. Moulton*

Out of curiosity, he turned to previous pages. A few terse comments summed up the lifetimes, joys, and sorrows of the family and laid raw the courage and pain of this pioneer family as they moved westward. His brief glance caught faded hard-to-read Spencerian writing:

Samuel Fuller, doctor from London, England, on the Mayflower. Borne in 1580, died 1633 of smallpox. Active in establishing Government. Separatist community in Leiden. Helped write Compact. Married (Alice Glascock, Agnes Carpenter, Bridget Lee, mother of children). Daughter: Mercy, 1627. Son: Samuel, 1629. Church deacon, Plymouth Tax Assessor.

A scribbled note in the margin:
3 sons, 3 daughters. One infant son born / died in three days.

The good doctor was awestruck. Samuel Fuller family of the Mayflower! He turned back to the current page and noted:

Samuel Fuller, from New York, married Lucinda Koontz,
(*Ohio and Indiana* had been scribbled near the margin with a thick-leaded pencil.)   *Charlotte, 1852*
          Emily, 1854

Dr. Moulton smiled. Soon they'll be writing Eugenia for Princess Eugenia of Spain – now Empress Eugenie and married to Napoleon, the Third. He whistled through his teeth with this information and had just turned away when Sam placed an oil lamp on the table and announced that dinner of sorts was on the kitchen table.

"Whatever it is, Sam, will be a welcome feast. This has been a day with little time for sustenance of the body," as he put his hand on his stomach, turned, and moved towards the kitchen with Sam. Charlotte and Emily were already seated on a bench and had their spoons in hand, ready to dip into the hearty soup as soon as the blessing was said and Ginny, the wife of one of the hired hands, brought hot bread to the table.

She was about to take some broth, tea, and a piping biscuit to Lucinda, but Sam took the tray from her and said, "You all go ahead. I'll be taking this to Missus Fuller. Besides, I want to get a fresh peek at our little princess." He turned back a moment later to say, "And John, your horses have been cared for and stalled. You'll be staying here tonight, and we'll see you off in the morning. I'll be back in a couple of jiffs."

Charlotte said the blessing. It was short. "Thank you for our food. Thank you for our home. Thank you for our sister. Thank you for everything." And the feast began.

The Fuller Homestead

COMMEMORATING
The Lincoln-Douglas Debate
KNOX COLLEGE   1858-1958 GALESBURG, ILLINOIS

" . . . there is but one path to peace . . . allowing each State to decide for itself whether it wants slavery or not."
—Douglas

Joint Debate Oct. 7th 1858

" . . . he is blowing out the moral lights around us, when he contends that whoever wants slaves has a right to hold them."
—Lincoln

The Lincoln-Douglas Debate
1858

Eugenia was in her favorite spot – on Papa's shoulders astraddle his neck. Sam raised his arms and held her hands, securing and balancing her, as he walked ever so carefully among his neighbors, new settlers, and folks from all around Knox County who were at Old Main for a history-making day. Mr. Douglas and Mr. Lincoln would soon begin their debate, and everyone wanted to have a good view of the men and, at the same time, be able to wander back a little when children fussed or they themselves grew tired of standing in one place.

Eugenia reached inches above her head for leaves that were almost touching her. The colors of the leaves on the big oaks and maples had changed and she grabbed first at a red leaf, then a gold. They were soft and smooth and cool to the touch and were still clinging tightly to the branches. Sam set down a large basket of food fixins', pulled a curvy oak leaf for her, and put it in her outstretched hand. Some ladies who had gathered around for conversation and support while their men roamed the campus, looked on and smiled approvingly. Lucinda, Sam's wife, was one of them. She and the daughters joined him and they found a long, rough-hewn log bench on an improvised mound, raised just enough for easier viewing, where they could sit, hear, and see in comfort. The air was crisp; gusts of wind whipped the women's skirts and leaves swirled around on the ground, occasionally making dense piles that became boisterous toys as children jumped into them.

The levity was contagious. Bands from Knoxville and Quincy filled the air with "My Country 'Tis of Thee," and girls from Lombard College gave small paper flags to anyone with an extended hand. Voices were raised from time to time among the menfolk arguing loudly whether Douglas or Lincoln would be Illinois' next senator, and every so often, a sonorous voice interrupted with, "Gentlemen, keep it civil," or "Respect our famous guests," or "Remember that women are present." A dust-up happened down the road and was stopped right after the first couple of blows. Mr. Fuller hied over to the spot to make sure his hired hands weren't involved. He wished the program would start. People needed to settle down. Many of the women were just plain tired from the early morning rush to prepare food, get the children ready, and make the bumpy, uncomfortable ride to Galesburg. Some, finally comfortable, even nodded off, only to be roused by the chill of the day when clouds blotted the sun, or when infants stirred in their arms. Still, the air was festive and everyone knew that this would be a story to recount over and over in years to come.

A rousing cheer went up when the officials and guests climbed through a window and settled themselves on the makeshift stage above the doors of Old Main. The awkward entrance drew laughter, and after an explanation by one of the organizers, Mr. Churchill, that the regular doors couldn't be opened because of the improvised stage, there was more laughter. Mr. Lincoln joked that he had just finally come through Knox College, and appreciative comments rippled through the huge audience.

"This is going to take a long time," said Sam. "I've been talking to some of the people in charge. First, Mr. Lincoln will speak for a while – an hour and a half, really, and then Mr. Douglas will have a turn for a couple of hours, and then Mr. Lincoln will have a half hour or more to try to turn Douglas' comments his way. We have a basket of food here and sweaters when the air chills, but when you get tired, Lucinda, or the girls get grumpy, let's be on our way. There's a big crowd here – must be thousands of people from all around, even as far away as Chicago – and they will never miss us. Both our wagon and carriage are out in the far field, so there won't be a ruckus when we go. In that case, we'll take the carriage, and Amos and Josiah will be in charge of the wagon's return."

"Oh, let's stay as long as we can, Sam. It is such an important event. I was just thinking that maybe Mr. Lincoln would like to come to our place to rest after the speeches. There's plenty of room if he would stay overnight. If you get a chance, ask him. Some of our neighbors would like to come over and talk to him, too, if he's not too tired."

"That sounds appropriate – very appropriate. I'll ask around, but I heard tell that Mayor Sanderson has invited him for dinner and sleeping over. If George Churchill's right, I'm thinking that it will be most politic for Mr. Lincoln to do it. I'll see if any other plans have been made for the next day or so. Even if he can't join us, he will know that he's welcome and will perhaps come on his next trip to Galesburg."

"Well, just in case, I can take the children and drive the wagon home early and we can have the fixins' all made up by the time the speeches are over and you bring him home to us. It's good that we brought both the wagon and the carriage."

"Well, we'll see. I know you have your mind set. Now best to just relax and hear what they have to say. Charlotte and Emily, come sit between us and be very attentive and quiet."

"Ladies and Gentlemen! Now on this beautiful Indian summer day, we are all gathered here at Knox College – a great, auspicious background for this occasion, to hear two very important men tell us how they will help us when they are senators of our great state of Illinois. Of course, only one will have the title of senator, but we all know that these two men love Illinois and are devoted to its people. So on this momentous date of October 7, 1858, let me introduce our speakers, and after that, we will set the protocol for the speeches we are about to enjoy."

Eugenia was cradled in her mother's blanketed arms by then and was struggling to keep her eyes open. Soon, even with the occasional crescendoing voices of the speakers, she drifted off to sleep, still grasping her leaf, and as befits a child of less than two, heard not one word that Mr. Lincoln and Mr. Douglas said.

Old Main, Knox College, Galesburg, Illinois

Good Water in the Well
1859

"I just hit sand, Mr. Fuller."

"Good – better than rock – keep going – God willing, the sand will get wet pretty soon and you'll have tough going for a while, and then you're going to see a really happy sight, Amos."

There was no answer from below except for the rhythmic scraping of sand or shale and then a plop into the bucket as the digging continued. "Pull her up again, Mr. Fuller," and without a word, the rope straightened, grew taut, and then began to lift the heavy load of rock chunks, dirt and sand to the surface of the ground. Mr. Fuller eyed the sand on top of the bucket. There was a difference already in the sand – difference in coarseness, difference in color. He grabbed a handful and let it sift through his fingers. Soon they would hit the underground spring. He unloaded the bucket onto the growing pile nearby and lowered it into the hole again.

"A few more times will do it, Amos."

"Want to take a wager, Mr. Fuller?" came Amos' reply with a voice muffled by the depth and the narrowness of the pit.

"No, Amos, you know I'm not a gamblin' man, but if I were, I'd wager five – no, three more loads."

"That'd put us at almost twenty-seven feet, sir—not far for a well, sir, but my back and arms would be grateful." Amos stopped to cough and spit. Repeated heaves and coughing stopped all conversation.

"Hey, spit in the bucket, Amos! Don't be contaminatin' my well, already! You hear?"

"You shure are persnickety, Mr. Fuller, but I spoz you're right. You're a right smart man." There was a soft plunk again on the bottom of the bucket, and the scraping of sand against shovel produced a few heavy solemn plops and then the rhythmical pattern began again.

"It's gettin' heavy t' lift – the shovel of sand, I mean. I mean, it's real heavy and my arms can't lift much. I must be getting plumb worn out."

"The sand is pulling water with it. You're getting to the end of the job. Thank the Lord!"

The bucket was lifted, and the return drop carried a plug of tobacco and a mug of hot coffee. Amos looked up. "Thanks, Miz Fuller, for the coffee. You are some picture. You two are framed against the blue sky and sunshine. You're a picture of hope, I can tell you."

"Thank you Amos," called Mrs. Fuller, as she leaned a bit further over the pit. "Coffee will help for the minute, but soon as you come up out of there, dinner's ready!" Then she picked up Eugenia who was tugging at her skirt, heisted her onto the left hip, and walked back to the house with Emily and Charlotte who were both fascinated and terrified at the big, gaping hole in the ground with a familiar voice coming up from it.

Two more loads and the water trickled onto Amos' boot. "You should be a gamblin' man, Mr. Fuller. If you'd wagered – even for work time on the farm, I'd be owin' you, sir!"

The call was passed on to other work hands and family along with – "He hit water!" – "Amos just struck water!" – "Git ready, everybody, we'll have dinner soon!" – "Yea for Amos!"

Soon, Amos – wet, mud spattered, sweaty, and smiling – was pulled to the surface and Mr. Fuller hugged and jostled him as he undid the knot at Amos' waist. "Good job – good job! I couldn't have done it better myself. Fellas, let's put this tin cover over it and weight it down with those rocks over there. Come now, Amos, get cleaned up and change into fresh duds that Mrs. Fuller has for you, and let's eat. It's time to praise the Lord and celebrate."

Amos went over to the cistern and drew up some water – stagnant and smelly compared to what he had just tasted! As he washed, he planned the next day's work. He'd clean up around the pit, sink the pump, and finish it off at the top so nothing could fall in. Tired and hungry as he was, he could hardly wait to get started. He heard the call to supper where the family and all the hired hands would sit down to a feast and say grace and pass the dishes around and around for seconds and thirds. He cleaned the mud off his shoes and headed straightaway for the kitchen. In the back of his mind, though, was the scene he knew he would see the next evening or so when the well was finished and the pump was primed and spewing out clear, pure water. Everyone would hug him and jostle him and make great remarks that because of him – Amos – there was good water in the well at the Fuller Homestead. "I am Amos – almost famous," he hummed to himself.

A symbol of settled stability

Mesopotamia in Illinois – Eugenia's Homeland

People all around talked about Galesburg being Mesopotamia, a reference to the Cradle of Civilization in Biblical times. The citizens relished the idea that Galesburg, located in a rich, fertile agricultural area between the Mighty Mississippi and the Illinois Rivers could be so aptly compared to the land of Mesopotamia located between the Tigris and Euphrates Rivers. It was even written in the tracts that were sent out to encourage others to emigrate to this land of milk and honey. Milk and honey, literally. The soil was dark and fertile, the area had expanses of flat land for plowing and harvesting, and both people and animals prospered. The Illinois and the Mighty Mississippi bounded the span of land, so once crops had been gathered, it was easy to ship them on to other areas for profit. Then the powers that be politicked for the railroad to go through Galesburg in 1854 and later on into Chicago. That was even better – for shipping products, for receiving furniture and equipment, for traveling, and for importing workers, such as the Swedes and the Irish to do heavy labor as businesses grew. Prices boomed. Lots that sold on Main Street for forty dollars at the town's inception in 1837 were seven thousand dollars by the time Eugenia was born in 1857.

Change occurred quickly. Earnest Calkins emphasized that by 1880, "... there were the makings of a small-town aristocracy as exclusive as it dared to be in a community so small and interdependent." A lower class of citizenry was born because of the differences in the cultures, economic status and education levels and was in distinct contrast with the original settler status, living on the north side of town, money lining pockets, religious affiliation, and levels of prosperity among the farmers. Rev. Gale tried very hard to keep his power and to prevent other religions from getting a toehold. The community was about evenly divided between Presbyterians and Congregationalists along with a good number of Universalists. The divisions caused serious consequences in the community. In the end, Rev. Gale personally lost out – with the college and with the religious control, even though he tried to pack the board of trustees with people who agreed with him, including his own son. Jonathan Blanchard, a brilliant protégé who had begun teaching at age fourteen and a half, exerted more and more influence on the college community and townsmen and became the second president of Knox College. He was charismatic but, oh, so strict! He was a foe of slavery, ales, cards, secret societies (Masons), gambling, blasphemy, Sabbath breaking, and not walking with the church. His sermons were long and threatening.

Financial panics occurred in the East. Fortunes were lost. More people read about the land of milk and honey and Mesopotamia in Illinois became a household term. Why? The financial woes happening all over the country did not affect Galesburg except for one aspect. Pioneers who had sold their homes in the East found that the new buyers, hit hard by the economy, were unable to make their payments. That factor did make a hardship on investors in Galesburg, but the community was just that and entered into agreements to help their neighbors survive and prosper. Most of the men had several ways to make a living. One might be a farmer, a lawyer, a surveyor, a postmaster, and involved in real estate all at the same time. Business was done on the go rather than in a personal office.

Historical references indicate that The United States Census in 1850 found many people living in the Galesburg area on the edge of poverty, but the Census in 1860 showed prosperity in both land ownership and personal items like large houses similar to those back East and increased values of possessions. Population increased rapidly, fine horses and cattle grazed the lands, and there was increased focus on education with the addition of Lombard College near the already famous Knox College. By 1870, the Census showed that bank accounts flourished, and most residents were convinced that they were or could become physically healthy, wealthy in real estate and inventions, and, with the advancements in railroad travel, had expedited shipping as their perennial monetary back-up.

Galesburg earned another Mesopotamian reference as the Seat of Learning in the area because both Lombard College and Knox College earned high praise from academics in the United States. Women were offered equal educational opportunities, and the astute alumni began to be acclaimed with prestigious positions throughout the nation.

Even in Mesopotamia, even in Galesburg, dark clouds gathered. There was talk of war, of states maybe seceding, of the pros and cons of slavery. Men gathered around the mail post in the general store and argued their views, views that ranged from polite questions to fisticuffs when talk turned to Democrats and Republicans, and especially our new President, Abraham Lincoln. Here, there was no middle ground. The President was either hated or beloved. Religious precepts disappeared when offending political comments were expressed or even hinted. Another term that raised hackles and voices instantly was the word abolition. Most Galesburgers were for it, but folks stopping by from other parts of the county – especially around Knoxville, the county seat – could not contain their anger and belief that the country was being destroyed, and some were willing to tussle and roll around on the floor to win their arguments.

Still, life went on. Chores were endless: cows to be milked, butter to be made, cattle, horses, sheep, hogs, and chickens to be fed – most of it about daylight and again before sunset. There were fruits and vegetables to harvest, followed with canning hundreds of jars for winter food – there was no end to it. Yes, there were hired hands who worked long hours, but children were farm assets, too. After age seven, Eugenia and her sisters wondered, "Is this what life is to be forever?"

Talk of War
1861

The fastest way to hear the news was to go to church on Sunday. Prayer meetings on Wednesday nights during the summer months was a good pipeline, too, for those living in close riding distance. For sure, though, the ringing of church bells on Sunday morning, and the strong mandate to be there, brought neighbors and relatives together for morning services to the Lord, followed often by a general community meeting, pot-luck dinners, ice cream socials or box suppers. This was a time for passing the news, a time for the fellows to spark the girls, a time for courting, a time for shaking hands on deals.

The news on Sunday in early April was sure to be solemn. Eugenia and her sisters were unusually quiet in the carriage, following the example of their parents. When they arrived in the churchyard and put their horses in the corral, people smiled and nodded. Nobody talked.

Parson Weaver was surprised to have the floor and everyone's attention without even asking for it. In her own thoughts, Eugenia imagined herself to be in charge. First the greeting, then the hymns – with all the verses – then the prayer with choruses of Amens at the end, and then the sermon. Oh, dear! The sermon! No matter how short, it would be too long!

Parson Aaron Weaver was new and he was different. Some people mumbled openly that he was too soft and never mentioned going to hell. Eugenia liked him right away. He looked her in the eye sometimes when he talked. He didn't yell. He didn't talk long either. Today, he sounded sad. He looked sad as he stood behind the pulpit that held his spread-out Bible.

Then something unheard of happened. Parson Weaver stepped away from the pulpit, pulled a chair from the side of the dais, sat down and faced the assembly with, "My friends, my countrymen, we are about to be in a civil war."

Stunned silence. Not because the statement was made – something taken for granted – but because of the Parson's behavior. "Before long," he began, "each of us will have to make a decision of what is right and what is wrong, follow through with that decision and be ready to face God with the consequences."

Stunned silence. Not a cough or baby's whimper. Eugenia's father described it later as a time to reach inside the heart and see what we're made of. Having to stand up and be counted wrenched our souls, he told others as they recalled the scene.

From the back of the room came a voice, quivering with anger. "You're our spiritual leader. It's your duty to tell us what we should do. That's why we're here. We need guidance and resolve and courage."

"I pray to God that I am guiding everyone today to think seriously of how you are going to support President Lincoln, preserve our country, and aid our boys who will go to war but may not come home. They should not die in vain. Regardless of how we feel today in this room, war will come. Soon. So let's talk. Mr. Latham, you started to say something."

Conversations began and carried on long past the regular meeting time and into the following week. By meeting time on the following Sunday, war had been declared.

The Wagon Load of Hay
1862

Rain splashed against the window in spats and the wind jostled its frame. Eugenia lay quietly in bed and wiggled her toes to make sure they were still there. Dawn was slow in coming, so her mind's eye enjoyed the wallpaper and the pictures on the wall. Especially one picture of sheep in a pasture. She shivered a little and pulled the quilted comforter closer to her chin and listened. There were those familiar sounds again. She had been wakened twice this week with them. Not loud, no, but muffled as of low grown-up voices and cranky cries of children not ready to call the night a day. The axles of the wagon creaked as it passed the house. She could hear the sounds in spite of the rain. She remembered that the wagon loaded with hay had been placed in the barn last night in case it rained and ruined the hay, her father had said. Then he had unhitched the horses and they wandered off into the pasture instead of being placed in their stalls.

Why would Amos be taking a load of hay anywhere when it was still dark and stormy? "I will ask him," she thought. She had already asked her mother about the night noises, but got a no-answer answer. Why wouldn't people tell her straight out what was happening? Why did father turn out his fine horses from their barn stalls on some nights and put cows in them instead? He said it was because the cows gave better milk next morning when they were kept inside at night. "Then why don't you do that every night?" she had asked. Wasn't it important to get more milk every morning? "Genie, you are just full of questions" was the common response.

And the neighbors didn't have a basement in their barns – with steps leading down from the barn floor. She knew because she'd heard Amos and Papa talking about it. And they didn't have a walkway – a corridor,

Papa called it – from the basement to the kitchen in the house, either. "It's all very strange and curious," she murmured to herself.

The wind turned in another direction and the rain fell gently on the window. Eugenia's musings turned into that delicious feeling between being awake and going to sleep.

When she awakened again, the rain was gone and the sun was shining on her face. Dreams of the storm and the wagon loaded with hay were gone as she reached for her satin robe she had received a couple of days ago on her fifth birthday. "What a pretty shade of blue. It matches the birds in the wallpaper. It is magnificent. Magnificent." Feeling how her mouth changed when she said the word was fun. When her father taught her the word last night, he asked her to say the syllables slowly and concentrate on her mouth. Mag (lips together and then open), ni (pull back on the lips), fi (let the breath come between the teeth), cent (do a hissing sound with the lips and teeth and end sharply with a t sound – tongue against the front teeth) "Magnificent! That is my new favorite word."

Eugenia made her bed, put her magnificent doll on the pillow and her magnificent robe on a hanger, dressed herself in a magnificent skirt and blouse and went downstairs.

Right away, she headed for the privy and waved to her mother who was working in a garden nearby. She greeted her mother a few minutes later with a question. This style of greeting had become a family joke. Always, Eugenia had questions. "Mama, why are the clothes still on the line from yesterday? See, they're all wet from the rain last night. Did you forget they were here? Look at the quilt! It's sagging almost to the ground. And the clothes! They're still dripping!"

"No need to fret, Genie. See – the sky is clear – isn't it beautiful – and the sun will soon dry out everything. It's perfectly all right. Charlotte and Emily have gone on to school. Are you ready for pancakes and jelly?" They raced each other to the screen door and the real day started for both of them. After breakfast, Eugenia stood on a stool and washed the dishes. Using a rag, she cleaned a plate and then slid it into another dishpan full of clear water. Then she washed and rinsed another plate or mug. She was very careful because dishes were hard to come by and breaking something would be so disappointing to everyone. It seemed there were more dishes than usual this morning. "Why do we have so many dishes and cups to wash, Mama?"

"Oh, Genie. We had some very interesting company last night."

"Then where are they now?"

"Well, well... They are on a mission and couldn't stay long. As usual, don't try to wash the pots and pans. I'll take care of them while you are dusting the front room." Genie made a face that her mother didn't see. "Why do I always feel this way when people don't answer my questions," she asked herself. "I get answers that aren't answers at all."

An hour or so later, Eugenia sat on a kitchen stool and watched her mother prepare the noon meal for the men who worked for Father. There was hammered steak with thick gravy and mashed potatoes and some green beans that Mama had cooked a long time ago and put into jars to save for meals like this. The smell of hot cornbread filled the room and Eugenia breathed in the fragrance as if she were savoring violets that she sometimes picked in the woods a little ways from the house.

Most of the men washed their hands with water from the rain barrel under the eaves, stomped their boots on the step, and came in through the back door of the kitchen, but Amos and her father came in through an opening in the pantry. It really didn't look like a door at all. She knew that the walkway led to a basement that tunneled all the way to the barn and most of the time, the opening there was covered with a cellar door and hay. Her father said that it was a fine short cut from the barn to the house and especially so when blizzards came in the winter and the snow piled high around the house. This corridor was the safest place to be, he said, when the tornados came, and she knew that was true because she and her sisters Emily and Charlotte, along with her parents and hired hands, had spent anxious hours there several times when the dark funnel clouds raged toward the ground. Eugenia was used to seeing her father – and sometimes

Amos – enter the house by using the short cut. At the moment, both men looked very tired, and she thought she saw them give nods to the other men – nods that were like a signal or a greeting. Why? Hadn't they all been working together on clearing the brush that morning?

Sweaty and tired, the men sat down to eat with compliments to Mama who blushed and accepted the kind words with grace. She then joined Eugenia at a small table at the far end of the kitchen. Mama's goal was to have the men feel they had privacy and could eat as they liked, but there were special rules for the women folk and that included five-year old girls. They listened, though, as the men began to talk about the war that had started more than a year ago and was getting bloodier with every report that came their way. Harvey Monson had gotten word that his cousin had been killed in the Shiloh battle. He choked on his food and turned away to clear his throat. The men made various comments to avoid a heavy silence that often occurred when someone at the table knew a soldier who had been killed. "God bless his soul." "He was one of God's chosen." "Amen!" "Praise the Lord." Josiah kept his head down as two of the young men quietly talked to each other of joining up soon. Josiah, with his lame leg, would be a danger to others, but he was going to figure out what he could do to help.

Eugenia gave her mother 'The Look' that always meant an argument was about to explode. It did. "I think God must be the meanest person in the whole world..."

"Genie, shush! Shush!"

"I don't care, Mama. That's what I think. This war is going to..."

"That's enough! Not one more word. Not one!" Eugenia saw her mother's forehead crease and her shoulders drop. "Mama feels the same way I do," she thought. "She does. Why doesn't she just say so? When I grow up, I'll say what I think is right and no one is going to shush, shush me."

About the time the men finished their cake and began moving towards the door, Mrs. Holcomb – the wife of one of the young men who worked for Father – arrived by horseback, and came straightaway in to clear the table and do all the dishes and pots and pans from the big meal. This was such a help for Mama who would have to put a light supper on the table in a few hours. Not to mention the relief that Eugenia felt. Doing the morning dishes was her job – but not the other times. All of a sudden, she felt like a real princess. She decided to go to her room upstairs, lie on her bed and play her pretend game of being grown up. Dreaming soon followed.

Laughter and easy conversation floated up the stairs and when Eugenia heard the voice of Mrs. Stowe – a favorite visitor – she ran down and ecstatically hugged her mama and Mrs. Stowe. Mama refilled their cups with tea and gave a cup to Eugenia. How grownup. This was much better than her pretend game. Soon the adults talked about Mrs. Stowe's book and the widening influence it was having on the abolitionist movement and the war. Their fingers worked busily on a quilt that was more than half finished. "Mama, why do you work most every day on a quilt? We have so many already. And how do you figure out which colors to use and which pictures to make?"

"Genie, my sweet child. You ask so many questions. We're making quilts for fun and to help other people who might need them. One day soon, you and Emily and Charlotte can make one. That reminds me. The girls should be home any minute. Do you want to run meet them?"

Image from a vintage greeting card

Flying Geese Pattern

North Star Pattern

Let time roll back and imagine this Fuller Homestead in its heyday – long before the bronze plaque stating Freedman was attached above its doorway and long before it began to disintegrate. This picture of it was taken in 1977-78, but it was built in the 1850s and the house was a character of strength and nobility in the countryside. Orchards and forests were in the back; a family cemetery amid a clearing was established on one side of the house, and barns and farmland extended on the other. Set in the middle of nowhere, it was a welcome sight to an occasional traveler and a Mecca to slaves escaping from the South and espying quilts spread across the clothes lines denoting a temporary safe haven.

Eugenia's parents were likely evasive about the many visitors that came and went under the darkness of night because the penalties for helping slaves escape were high. The spoken word – even of children who made comments in all innocence – could have dire consequences. Page 10 of <u>Hiram Revels in Illinois</u> by Marvin Litvin lists excerpts from THE REVISED STATUTES OF ILLINOIS approved March 3, 1845. The following is in Chapter 54 under the head of "Negroes and Mulattoes."

> Section 8. Any person who shall hereafter bring into this State any black or mulatto person, in order to free him or her from slavery, or shall directly or indirectly bring into this State, or aid or assist any person in bringing any such black and mulatto person to settle and reside therein, shall be fined one hundred dollars on conviction and indictment, before any justice of the peace in the county where such offense shall be committed. (Relevant Sections 9, 10, 12 and 13 follow.)

The Drownings
Josiah's Story

When I seen them there in the water, I knowed they wuz goners. Their hair was kinda spread out on the water and a little red bow perked on the side of one head. And they was face down and just afloatin'. The cows I was after was on the other side of the pond, but I clean forgot about 'em.

Even though I knowed it wouldn't do no good, I grabbed a long stick and tried to hook into the closest one. No use. Their bodies were kinda slanted down into the water which was so clear I could see that one of the girls had lost a shoe but still had her stockin's on. O my precious Jesus. If only I could swim. "Get help," Jesus told me. "Get help." And I wheeled 'round in the slippery, early mornin' grass and headed for the house on the hill across the meadow.

I kept slippin', and havin' to drag my lame leg didn't help none. "Mr. Sweazy!" I yelled. "Mr. Sweazy!" No answer. Gol dam and damnation – 'scuse me. But – "Hey! Help! Come here!" I pulled my leg and pushed ahead and finally got Mr. Sweazy's attention. "Mr. Sweazy! Mr. Sweazy!" He was out in the last shed by the pigs.

"Yeh? Yeh? What's the matter, Josiah? What's the matter? Something wrong at Mr. Fuller's?" He started comin' towards me, and when he seen me almost face to face in a cluster of sheep that seemed surprised but didn't panic, he ran towards me.

He got really alarmed and there was scaredness in his voice. "What's the matter? Did one of the cows fall into the pond?"

"No sir – no sir." I was just gasps now. My head was ready to bust and I didn't know how to tell him. My tongue just moved on its own. "No sir – not the cows, sir. Your granddaughter and her little friend. They're face down in the water – I think they're dead!" And then I fell down in front of him and cried. Face down in the meadow grass and Queen Anne's lace and dock and goldenrod. I laid there and heard shouts and cries as Mr. Sweazy alerted farm helpers, and they went runnin' to the pond.

I didn't need to look there anymore. I knowed what they'd see. This grand, natural spring made a great waterin' hole for the livestock in a low part of the pasture field, but it was a killer hole, too. Only a couple months ago, a young colt had slipped into the water and drowned and now these two beautiful little girls!

They used to follow me and tease me 'bout my leg, but they never meant to be mean. They wuz just full of life like any little girls – neither one was over four.

My breathin' started to come back, but I just laid there for a long time. I knowed I should get up and go down to see what was goin' on, but I knowed what was goin' on, and so I couldn't go. I just wanted to lay flat on the ground and sink right into it. Where was Jesus? Where was Jesus for those two little girls? I didn't even know their names. Sorrowful sounds, wailin', cries, screams drew closer and louder as the little girls were carried into the house. Mr. Fuller walked up to me where I was still layin' knee deep in the flowers.

"Josiah," he said. "You did the right thing. You came for help when you knew there was nothing you could do. You got people out there right away. You are a good boy. Let me help you up and let's go home."

We had walked nearly half to the mile to his house when I struggled with myself and blurted out, "Those were just little girls. They didn't hurt nobody. How could Jesus let that happen?"

Mr. Fuller was quiet a long time. "Maybe he didn't hear me, maybe he's mad about my askin'," Josiah thought to himself.

Finally – and in a tired voice, Mr. Fuller said, "I have no answer for you. It is a mystery. It is easy for us to ask the question, and I have done it many times. Sometimes we lose the faith and then something else happens, and we get it back again. I know one thing, though. When we get to the house, you and I will double check the covered part around our well. We have to make sure it's safe. A catastrophe set up by nature is bad. We don't want to compound it by careless acts of man. Remember this, Josiah, and keep an eye out on the farm – and on my girls. I wish, I really wish I had answers for you about God – about Jesus, about the universe. I did when I was twenty or so. I had all the answers. Now I know very little – next to nothing. Yet, we must try to keep faith with what we've been taught.

"Now come in for a mug of coffee and a piece of Miss Lucinda's pie." Mr. Fuller now faced the dilemma of joyfully thanking God for his blessed Charlotte and Emily and Eugenia, who were looking at books on the sofa near the window, and at the same time telling his wife about the tragedy. Something like this happened to a family several years ago before they settled here, and Lucinda was inconsolable for months. She was so happy now, and he was about to send her back into the dark period neither one could tolerate. Having Josiah in the kitchen would help.

The two men gave the bad news – Sam, trying to be calm and keep a steady voice, while Josiah's voice interrupted and varied from a choked wail to high-pitched tones of desperation. Lucinda surprised them both. She clasped her hands and, at several points in the telling of the story, pulled her apron to her face, but she remained calm – for the children, perhaps, or because difficult pioneer life had changed her.

The ups and downs of the conversation had drawn the girls' attention to the kitchen, and they'd left the books behind to find out what was going on. Lucinda pulled them close as if never again to let them out of her sight. "Josiah, we can't blame God. It wasn't His will to punish innocents. I just don't believe that. And, no, you can't blame yourself, just because you got out to the fields a mite later than usual. It was a terrible accident, that's for sure, and you did the best you could after you saw the situation."

Josiah would not be comforted. His shoulders shook. His face was contorted. He hammered his fist on his knee. "Why do bad things happen to people who are good, and evil people like the Hoskin family across the crick get life their way?" No one answered. Lucinda removed the kettle from the stove and brewed more tea. Silence hung heavy in the kitchen.

Eugenia was five, going on six. The scene made an indelible impression; questions were stored somewhere in her brain and, as she grew older, visited her consciousness over and over. Questions about justice, fairness, and God's Will would influence her entire life.

The Schoolhouse
1863

Come September, in her Sunday best and an old Perry's spelling book in one hand and carefully carrying a wooden basket covered with a cloth napkin in the other, six year-old Eugenia picked her steps carefully as she went down the steep hill, crossed the log planks bridging Fuller Creek with some trepidation and scurried up the hill with her sisters, Charlotte and Emily, to discover her new world of the schoolhouse. From one room to several stories and within several capacities, she was destined to spend most of her life within the walls of schoolhouses.

This particular schoolhouse stood on the top of a hill on the north side of what was called Fuller Road. The Fuller homestead was a good half-mile away and other families even further. The location had been a bone of contention among the distant neighbors for a while because people in each direction of the school were as determined as those in the other directions to have the school located closer to their own homes. Still, with Sam Fuller's convincing talking points and his willingness to supply some of the lumber and labor, there was general agreement and cooperation, and parents pitched in to help. Mr. Fuller made sure that a spring nearby was suitable for drinking water. He volunteered to help out in emergencies. He was a township trustee. He was a parent with three daughters. He was a farmer with the most land around. He was a god-fearing, educated man. He was a quiet power in the community.

The school set isolated in a clearing surrounded by timber and near a creek that bubbled eagerly in the summertime, grew hard enough to skate upon in the winter, and was a dangerous rushing torrent in spring and fall after cloudbursts and run-offs of thawing snow.

A woodpile lay in a corner outside the back door and most of the time was sheltered from the ravages of the weather. Just seeing it and realizing the daily rituals it required had to have been a symbol of dedication to teaching, since it was the teacher's job to lug the wood into the schoolhouse and keep the fireplace stoked. Chunks of coal were selected from the bucket near the fireplace, and pieces of wood from the dry kindling box helped the banked fire come to life. It was a dirty job. Only passing time would classify the duties as 'managing the environment of the workspace.'

During inclement weather, wet wood, a poor draft, or rain falling down the chimney caused the wood to smolder and smoke. Watery eyes and coughs of students followed. Whether the students would try to stifle the discomfort or outdo each other with giggles and exaggerated moans of distress – which delayed the recitations – depended upon the teacher's disciplinary control.

When rain fell, the roof nearly always leaked and sometimes the bucket containing the dipper and water drawn from the nearby spring had to be moved from a ledge in the back of the room up near the teacher's desk. That happened for two reasons. Water from the holes in that section of the roof leaked into it and for another, some of the older boys tracked back and forth, back and forth, back and forth from their seats to the water pail, not because they were thirsty, but because the weather made them bored and restless, and they considered such meandering an authorized mission. Sparring around with the dipper and carelessly drinking from it got even more water on the floor, and then no one wanted to go to the spring to replenish the water unless a friend went with him to help carry the pail back to class. The teacher knew that sending two boys for water meant that hours might pass (possibly near dismissal time) before there would be water for the remaining students. Moving the pail signaled no more drinks for the day without the teacher's permission.

The door stoop was a boulder that had been dragged from the nearby pasture field. The rock had been sunk into the ground and gave a flat appearance as one stepped from the ground to the stoop and on into the building that had been carefully constructed several years ago. The smooth surface of the rock was deceptive, though, because it became slippery when it was wet or glazed with ice.

The schoolhouse had six tall windows with wooden shutters. The expensive glass sometimes broke and had to be patched. If shutters were not securely latched, they often produced a rhythmic pattern of slamming against the wall of the school and then sliding toward the windows and deflecting or closing out the light.

Inside was the smell of the pine building itself, fragrant fire wood which had been stocked as a precaution against bad weather, acrid wood smoke from the fireplace embers, stale sweat from warm bodies in various stages of cleanliness from the days before, released gas from reluctant students who hoped to be sent outside, mixed with the smells of wet clothes, kerosene lamps, sandwiches in lids of lunch boxes, the oiled floor, and chalk. Of course, it was different in the spring and Indian summer days when windows were open and the movements of butterflies and bumble bees were monitored as they roamed around the room before they finally found their ways back outside. These creatures provided respite from the regular routines, and for some pupils acted as imaginary rescuers from the drone of the teacher's voice and student recitations. The hypnotic attractions caused more than one head to nod and rest on the desk. Sometimes, fresh flowers placed in a jar on the teacher's desk added a touch of beauty to the otherwise drab environment, and the fragrance wafted to the first two or three students sitting nearby.

The room was about thirty feet long and twenty feet wide. At the south end of it, near the entrance, was one seat and writing bench making a right angle with the rest of the seats. This space was occupied in the winter by two of the oldest boys in the school. At the opposite end was the teacher's desk, raised upon a platform half a foot from the floor. The fireplace was on the right, between the entrance and another door that led into a dark closet where the pupils put their outer garments and their dinner pails and baskets. This dark space also served as a punishment area for offending members of the school. Some didn't mind going into the closet in the mornings. They got their breakfasts by raiding dinner containers, and sometimes they had to be awakened by the teacher or other students because the closet was a warm dark place to nap after the hearty snacks. It soon became the rule that recalcitrants were placed by the teacher's desk in the mornings and foisted into the closet after the noon meal.

Directly opposite the fireplace was an aisle, two and a half feet wide, running up on an inclined floor to the opposite wall. On each side of the room were five or six long seats and writing desks. In front of these were low narrow seats called recitation benches for the abcdarians and others of that rank. In general, the older the scholar, the further from the front he was located. The girls sat on one side, the boys on the other. The windows behind the last seats were so low that a person traveling by could generally catch the curious glances of the students.

Such was the old school house at the time Eugenia first entered school in 1863. Subsequent changes were made in the appearance, but the "feel" she had of the school remained unchanged as the years passed and she progressed through her studies. Her older sisters, Charlotte and Emily, gave her confidence as she learned the routines.

The teacher was in charge of everything – cleaning the floor, bringing the water bucket, firing and emptying the fireplace, cleaning the lamps, patching the windows and blinds, teaching, examining, and occasionally giving lashes to rule breakers. Eugenia had mixed feelings about that. It was fine to be in charge, and she admired her teacher for knowing everything. But why, oh why, must the learned person also be in charge of all the chores? Some older boys and, once in a while, a parent came to school early or stayed late to help. Eugenia approved of that. "Someday, I will be a teacher. I will teach. I am not going to do all of those chores."

During her years at Mt. Joy School and beyond, Eugenia had several teachers and each one had special and "right" ways of doing things. One teacher hardly ever asked students to help or assigned duties to them. One involved the students in doing so many tasks that the teacher did little more than to keep everyone's tasks straight and teach. Another was so hateful that every job and lesson assigned to students was done with an undercurrent of resentfulness. Her very favorite teacher was Mary Allen West. She knew her students by first name right away and her presence made everyone feel ever so important. Later, as a teenager, Eugenia wrote in her diary that when she graduated, she would teach just like Miss Mary Allen West who was becoming a notable legend in her own time.

Born in 1837 to the large Nehemiah West family, leading pioneers in the early settlement of Log City, the precocious Mary Allen West began teaching at the age of thirteen at the suggestion of Knox College officials because she was too young to be admitted to college classes. She became a highly respected, innovative teacher, and was nominated and elected to the Knox County School Superintendent's position without any effort on her part except for being Mary Allen West who passionately believed that the problems of the universe could be solved with educating all the citizens, including the many black children escaping or freed from slavery, who would be encouraged to work with and care for others. Mary Allen had full community support, prompted even by some typical naysayers, perhaps because of her tireless, unflagging enthusiasm, exceptional knowledge, persuasive powers, and community connections. Hours that would have been considered free time by others involved missionary work with the Prairie Gleaners, official work with the Soldiers' Aid Society, activities with the Temperance Union, writing articles for educational journals, teaching large Sunday School classes at church in the morning and working with inmates in the afternoon at the newly instituted Galesburg Jail – and more. When questioned about how she was able to constantly interact and work for others, she demurred by explaining that she was having such a good time and that it wasn't so-called work at all.

Even with progress in other professions, teachers had the onus of doing everything in order to meet the requirements of the trustees of the schools. Not so for Eugenia. From her first year in school, she fantasized about how she would be in charge of the school. She would assign tasks to others so she could teach. She kept her dream, embellished it as the years went by and had a master plan in her mind for how she would someday run the school. She vowed she would not be one of the many examples she watched with mixed emotions. She often questioned her father, a school trustee, as to why teachers didn't stay long, why they were treated like grownups who had to be watched, why they had to do all the chores, and why they had to do everything the trustees required whether it was fair or not. She pitied the teachers – men and women – who had no homes of their own, but had to room and board with parents on a rotation basis. Their jobs never ended. They were with students or their parents all the time with little privacy, little power, little chance of doing anything else with their lives until the men went into law or other vocations and the women married. The only time for their own dreams was after dinner with the families, after preparing lessons, after the evening Bible study, after everyone went to sleep and then finally – a few hours to themselves before dawn. Why would anyone want to be a teacher and exist like that?

Mt Joy School

Typical Expectations for Teachers

RULES FOR TEACHERS
1872

1. Teachers each day will fill lamps, clean chimneys.

2. Each teacher will bring a bucket of water and a scuttle of coal for the day's session.

3. Make your pens carefully. You may whittle nibs to the individual taste of the pupils.

4. Men teachers may take one evening each week for courting purposes, or two evenings a week if they go to church regularly.

5. After ten hours in school, the teachers may spend the remaining time reading the Bible or other good books.

6. Women teachers who marry or engage in unseemly conduct will be dismissed.

7. Every teacher should lay aside from each pay a goodly sum of his earnings for his benefit during his declining years so that he will not become a burden on society.

8. Any teacher who smokes, uses liquor in any form, frequents pool or public halls, or gets shaved in a barber shop will give good reason to suspect his worth, intention, integrity and honesty.

9. The teacher who performs his labor faithfully and without fault for five years will be given an increase of twenty-five cents per week in his pay, providing the Board of Education approves.

Berry Picking
1864

Eugenia's bedroom, small as it was, was a treasure chest because of the window that looked out onto the fields. Branches of a huge gingko tree spread within inches of the window and made a secure hideaway in the springtime and summer. Eugenia leaned her elbows on the sill and pressed her face against the panes that had wavy marks in the glass held in place by small frames. Father had raised the window partway and put a stick under the window to hold it in place so that she could listen to the night sounds and get a breeze to air out the room. The best pleasure, though, was watching Mama and Papa Warbler feeding their babies in the early morning hours. The nest was in grabbing distance from Eugenia's hands, but she would never dare do such a mean thing to her friends who accepted her admiration without fear. "I must breathe gently and not move. Here comes Mama, again. She's got a long brown worm in her beak, and now look at how she and papa cut it into pieces and drop a bit into each baby's mouth. For such tiny babies, they have big mouths and open them very wide. I'll be so glad when they get real feathers. They're so strange looking – as if they're from a prehistoric world." The stage play was interrupted by the persistent call of "Genie, GENIE," from downstairs.

"Hurry. Eat your oatmeal, put on your stockings and shoes. Soon the sun will make it too hot for..."

"Berrypickin' again? You and Charlotte and Emily go... let me stay here with Brownie." Brownie perked up his ears and moved close to Eugenia.

"No, no, no. You must do your share. You love the jelly, don't you? Don't shirk."

"Mama, I'm not shirking. Really. The sun does something to my head and everything swims around me. I can't even see the berries, and I think I shall faint."

"I know. We've heard those pleas many times. It's early morning yet. You will be all right."

"But you stay too long. It's one more bush and then one more bush, and we end up staying for hours. May I please stay here?"

The berries grew best down by the creek side. The fruits were ripe and plump and filled with sugar water. The goal today was to pick four gallons – one for each person. When Genie protested that she was 'just a poor little girl,' the others laughed and said, "Your fingers are nimble. You can pick even faster."

When they reached the Spot for the day, the first priority was to scan the area for snakes, then wrap their skirts around their legs to keep the chiggers and bees away, then adjust the bonnets so their faces were shaded, and finally to put shoulder towels in place to wipe the stains from fingers and sweat from the face and neck. "We'll make this a race," Charlotte said to soothe feelings and get off to a good start. "Ready, set, go!"

The sounds of berries hitting the bottom of the buckets were rhythmic; soon the sounds were muffled by layers of berries and later, no sounds at all. Charlotte, Emily, and Mama enjoyed this time because they could banter and gossip and laugh. Time passed so fast for them, they always said. Not for Genie. The berries smelled so good – her mouth watered. She decided that eating every third berry was a delicious treat for her hard work. The sun rose higher and the rays against her bonnet and heavy skirts began to make her weak. The others used their towels frequently to wipe off sweat. Genie didn't do that. There was no sweat – just weakness – and then she tumbled into a heap, and her berry bucket rolled down over the bank. She was told later that Charlotte carried her to the creek, took off her shoes and stockings and put her feet in the clear, cold, bubbling water. Mama removed Genie's bonnet and placed a towel dripping with creek water on the top of her head. Emily held Genie's hand and kept saying, "Genie, you'll be all right, you'll be all right."

And she was, of course. Her berry picking for the day was finished. She pressed her toes against the small rocks in the cool water, and shade from an overhanging willow tree made her feel inside her skin again. Mama, Char, and Em went back to work, filled their buckets to the brim, and then took turns filling Genie's bucket while the others cooled off in the shade and sampled berries. Holding their skirts high, they waded in the creek and asked riddles of each other until Genie was strong enough to stand and walk. Mama and Charlotte carried two buckets each. Emily held onto Genie and adjusted her walking pace. Twice along the way, everyone stopped to rest and it was a great relief to finally walk through the back door and into the kitchen. Because the house was hot, too, they made sandwiches and went into the underground corridor walkway to eat. It was so cool, so dark, so comfortable; soon all four were napping. That is where Father found them when he and his hired hands came home for the noon meal and found only four gallons of berries on the table.

Cloud Pictures
1867

"Mama, please come play with me."

"I must finish churning and patting the butter. Then if time permits, perhaps we can take a walk and count the butterflies we see."

"Mama, when you were a little girl, did your mama play with you sometimes?"

"Genie, why do you ask?"

"Mama, quit answering my questions with questions! I just want to know if you were lonely when you were a little girl and if your mother ever had time to play with you and take away the lump in your throat and a feeling that something bad was about to happen?"

Mama stopped turning the handle and put the churn of half-made butter in the walkway of the inside corridor. When she took off her apron and checked the pins in her hair, Eugenia's face beamed crinkly smiles. "Oh, Mama, we're going to have fun. Let's go play cloud pictures." Suddenly, the day was so beautiful.

With Brownie between them, they lay on a grassy knoll a short ways from the house. Their faces turned up to the sky. "You go first, Eugenia. What do you see?"

"Ooh! I see a giant bird. Look, Mama, there. There, do you see? On this side is the head and there's the tail, and down there are the two legs and feet. See?" Time passed and each pointed out cloud pictures in the sky.

After a while, they agreed to close their eyes and just rest. The breeze had picked up and it caressed their faces and rustled their hair. The sun went into hiding and when they looked at the sky again, the huge white

cumulous puffballs were turning grayish blue. "It's time for us to go. It's going to rain soon." Still, they dawdled until little drops began to fall on them. They helped each other up. Eugenia did a handspring flip, stood on tiptoes, and clasped her mother's waist. "Mama, Mama, thank you for today. I love you so very much. Someday, when you are lonely and scared, I will remember this day, and we'll play cloud pictures and you'll feel better."

"This day is just as special to me. When you grow up and have your own family, we will always be together when we look at the puffballs in the sky. I dearly love you, my child." Mama's voice wavered and a choked sob escaped. Genie looked at her with new eyes. In a flash, she realized that inside, Mama was a little girl, too. She thought to herself that when she grew up, she wouldn't ever shut the little girl up inside her woman's body. Brownie barked. 'Time to go home. It's raining!'

Holding hands, they ran through the field and laughed as the rain dotted and then pelted them with drops. Brownie nipped at their heels, urging them to go faster, faster. It was a wonderful day that made lasting memories of the joy of finding cloud pictures, running together, feeling rain in their faces, and falling into Father's arms as he waited for them near the kitchen door. "What a happy life we have here! Such a happy life," he repeated. "God has truly blessed us here in North Henderson! This is all we need of heaven." The rain had stopped and the late afternoon sun glistened again.

Neighbor Haven pulled up in his rough-board wagon filled with young ladies moments later. Charlotte and Emily jumped to the ground, and both reached their arms up to Rosandra as they thanked her for the Youth's Companion meeting. The adults exchanged pleasantries and then Mama nodded to the girls who turned towards Mr. Haven. "Oh, and thank you, thank you, thank you for bringing us home, Mr. Haven. And thank you and Mrs. Haven for letting us visit your home. And thank you again for the pie." Their voices were so nearly alike that it wasn't clear who started the comments and who chimed in. Everyone laughed.

"Well, must be gettin' on. I still need to deliver Mary Beth and Phoebe to their homes, and then Rosandra and I'll be headin' home. Think the rain is over? Nice to see you neighbors again." Without hesitation, he called to his horse and was on his way.

"He's such a funny gentleman. He talks in such short clips and never waits for an answer. He stays straight on his own mind track," Mama said in a voice carrying a smile."

"For all of that, he's a fine man, a fine, decent farmer, and husband and father. He and Mrs. Haven are fine neighbors," added Father.

"We're fine people, too. Everybody says so," added Eugenia.

"So they do, little one, and we must be humble about that. If we become too proud and care about ourselves too much, we will be headed for some hard lessons. Anybody hungry?"

"Oh, yes – and here is the pie that Mrs. Haven sent to you. She said we contributed so much to our discussions today. And we brought two Youth's Companions home to share with you, and guess what, Genie? Char is changing her nickname to Sharlie. Guess who thought of it? Andrew. Andrew Haven. He's sweet on SHARLIE."

Charlotte clapped her hand across Emily's mouth. "Oh, Em, be quiet! You are such a noggle head."

Em continued, "Sharlie, Sharlie, Sharlie! Andrew fancies Sharlie!"

"You girls stop that – this minute – do you hear? Come help prepare supper. We're having fresh corn chowder, some salted cucumber slices, and maybe – just maybe, this delicious apricot pie!" Papa was already seated at the table.

The girls knew that teasing would have to wait 'til later, but the sparkles in their eyes and mischievous smiles would have told even a stranger that they were just biding their time to carry on their hilarity – at Charlotte's expense, albeit a willing victim.

Mama said a simple blessing and everyone murmured "Amen" before the conversations turned, as they did almost every evening, to answering Papa's questions about history, geography, mathematics or literature and trying to outdo each other with knowledge. Answering with a yes or no was not permitted without a further explanation that would show understanding of the question or the lack of it. Learning was a joy for all of them, and it brought such a satisfaction, they often said, to learn something new at the end of each day. "You'll make Lombard College proud of you," Papa predicted.

It was taken for granted that the girls would go to Lombard and then decide how to deal with the world. Each time they went into town, either to shop or to sell their garden produce, a trip had to be made to the Lombard College grounds. There, they could envision themselves matriculated into the program and imagine what they would do with their lives after they grew up and left the farm. Their very names, Charlotte and Emily for the Bronte sisters and Eugenia for Empress Eugenie had already set their parents' expectations. Their parents, relatives, and friendly neighbors sparked encouragement to be competitive along with the added energy of their own role models: Cousin Margaret, Mother Mary Bickerdyke, Mary Allen West, Mrs. Mary Gettemy and others who beckoned them.

Lombard College Campus, Galesburg, Illinois

Lombard College

Lombard's School Colors and Seal

Lombard College

Lombard College was founded in 1853 by the Universalist Church as the Illinois Liberal Institute. After Oberlin, Ohio, this was the first college in the United States to matriculate both sexes without prejudice. A major fire damaged much of the college in 1855, but Benjamin Lombard, an Illinois farmer, came to the rescue and rechristened it Lombard University. Later, the name was changed back to Lombard College. It was coeducational from its first funding and always reflected the Universalist philosophy. This is where the Charlotte, Emily, and Eugenia Fuller girls graduated with honors from a very sophisticated and advanced academic program in the late 1870s. This is where Abraham Brown, Eugenia's suitor, graduated in 1870. This is where David Starr Jordan inspired his students in 1873, including the Fuller girls, and who later became the founding President of Stanford University in 1891, and Eugenia's California mentor.

Jane Addams, in the 1928 ceremony, received an honorary degree when she presented the commencement class. Her early contributions to social reform for women resulted in the Nobel Peace Prize award. She was declared a citizen of the world, the champion of peace, and a friend and servant of humanity when she was honored at Lombard.

After the Crash of '29, Lombard fell onto hard times and after 1930 existed only through Knox County Archives and the thoughtful reminisces of its students. Still, mention Lombard College, and people come to attention whether they attended Lombard or not. The reputation lives on.

Pi Beta Phi Fraternity
1872

The evening of June 22, 1872, was most exciting. Eleven Lombard students met with a leader to establish a beta chapter as IOTA Chapter of I.C. Sorosis. Of the eleven charter members, three were Charlotte Fuller Risley, Eugenie Fuller, and Emily Fuller. All were aware of the awesome responsibilities of their involvement and took extra effort of marking their places in the social history of the day. Within a few years, the organization prospered quickly to nearly three hundred members and at the Indianola Convention in 1886, the chapter became ILLINOIS BETA.

This significant group had been preceded by two college women in 1865 who asked questions like "If the men can have fraternities, why can't we?" The answer was a resounding "We can and we will!" albeit they were careful to do the planning "behind closed blinds and in whispered words." Two years later, on April 28, 1867, eleven girls founded their organization with such secrecy and mystery that would make us laugh today. For instance, they wrote their constitution with "every other two letters being omitted... to insure secrecy." They decided upon a grip, but of course it was a secret.

With so many Greek clubs being formed in prestigious colleges during that time period, many questions arose about the propriety of such groups and whether such secrecy and social activities interfered with studying and taking college life seriously. There was talk, too, that it was fine for the men, but suspect on several levels for young women. For a while, fraternities and secret societies were the talk of the college town, especially on street corners when people came in to make purchases on Saturday. One such heated group discussion occurred outside the Union Hotel.

"We'll have you know that we are just not copying the men," defended one of Lombard's finest.

"Yes, you are!" said an antagonist. "If the men hadn't started this whole silly thing, you ladies wouldn't even consider it."

"Yes, it's on record here at Lombard that Abie Brown and some of his friends set up the Delta Theta Society, and he was president of it just like Emma Brownlee became president of the Beta's."

"Oh, yes, I remember reading about that group. 'Some energetic students' felt the need of such a group, and they met upstairs in my grandfather's store on Day Street. That group went through several name changes, too: Delta Theta, Delta tau Delta, then Lambda. Abraham Brown started and was president of the Erosophian Society, too, along about 1867 – a group that held debates and read essays as literary exercises at Lombard. Those "'Clever Boys,'" as they were called, really were, and they made the girls jealous because they wouldn't let them join."

"Yes, and that's about the time that the women set up the Zetecalian Society in the Library and met regularly there on Friday afternoons with the blessings of the faculty. See how competitive they were?"

"Well, you know that Abraham and Eugenia had been sweet on each other for years. So, truly, there could have been competition there, too."

"What do these groups do, anyway?"

"I hear that they're all about living by high standards, giving service to others, providing kinship to each other, and encouraging high intellectual, moral, and spiritual standards for generations to follow. Sounds very lofty."

"That's just what I've heard some of the men say about their groups."

"Sounds like they're building the country, not subverting it."

"Anyway, just because some of the men organized first doesn't mean that we can't. We're not trying to be like them. Anything they can do, we can, too. The goals are serious and require sacrifice and loyalty, and the desire to help others. We really want to do this. If the men can organize and pursue their goals, so can we!"

"You just proved my point. Case closed."

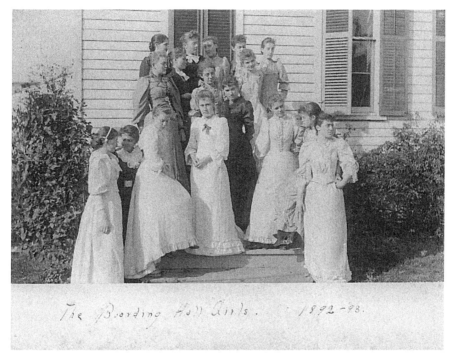

The Boarding Hall Girls. 1892-93.

A typical picture of the women students at Lombard

The Twenty-Second Commencement
June 19, 1877

Parents, uncles, aunts, cousins, classmates, neighbors, and faculty members gathered in the great room for the evening's orations and graduation certifications. George and Charles wore dark suits, white dress shirts and black ties, and the five young women wore white gowns, albeit various styles, along with purple sashes gathered at the waists. Clara, Emily, Eugenia, Lottie, and Ella sat in the front row on the stage, and the two men sat behind them on an elevated platform so that all could be seen equally well.

Near the grand piano was a large placard decorated with green and gold gingko leaves across the top. It read:

The Senior Class Members
graduating on June 20, 1877
from Lombard University are as follows:

George F. Baker,	Classical Course,	Galesburg
Charles C. Maynard,	Classical Course,	Canton
Clara Z. Edwards,	Literary Course,	Galesburg
Emily L. Fuller,	Classical Course,	N. Henderson
Eugenia Fuller,	Classical Course,	N. Henderson
Lottie J. Humphrey,	Scientific Course,	Tipton, Iowa
Ella McCullough,	Literary Course,	Galesburg

Audience members were dressed in their very best, and faces shone with bursting pride with the accomplishments of the seven graduates. Mr. and Mrs. Fuller multiplied their thankfulness as Charlotte, last year's graduate, sat between them, and Emily and Eugenia smiled at them from the seats of honor. "Three in one family," someone murmured, "and the word is that these two, like their sister, are already working on master's degrees."

Junior Class members ushered and handed programs adorned with petite green and gold ribbons to the guests who studiously read and reread and read again the precious contents. Across the top of the page was the motto

"WE ARE CONFIDENT WITH REFERENCE TO THE FUTURE" and beneath that was the listing of the graduates in the order of their evening's contribution. The program was about to begin!

First, there was a Piano Concerto selection from Chopin, a prayer of entreaty for the graduates, and more music that set a marching tone of victory. Then Clara spoke: "Ancient and Modern Amusements." Ella followed with "Culture versus Wealth." A string quartet followed these fine elocutions, and soon after, Lotti spoke on "The Study of History." George Baker then gave an oration on "The Continental Congress." An intermission sustained with music followed. Shortly after, Emily gave an essay on "Genius and Heroism," and C. C. Maynard followed with "The World Moves." Additional musical selections followed, including a sweet duet of Whispering Hope, and then Eugenia presented the Valedictory Address: "The Moral Element in Grecian Literature." Guests had been asked to hold their applause until the end and when it came, the response was raucous, expressive, and explosive, thus venting the pent-up energy of the long evening. The exultant march played again, softened for the benediction that praised the parents and families of these seven graduates, and then escalated as the men graduates received thumping handshakes along with leather bound Bibles, and the young women received bouquets of long stemmed flowers and brief kisses on their cheeks.

Eugenia blushed more so than usual when Abraham greeted her and brushed her cheek with a lip caress. "Abie, does tonight remind you of your special night here in 1870?"

"Of course, Genie, but this one is so much sweeter. I had no lines to remember tonight; instead, I basked in your loveliness for four blessed hours."

A brief "Ahem" from a faculty member broke the lovers' spell, and others stepped forward to congratulate Eugenia and move her gently towards the lavish reception in the Social Hall.

Papa, the Best Man in the World
September 13, 1882

They both knew his time was short. Genie tempted him with his favorite dessert that her mother had prepared. Warm raisin bread pudding flooded with freshly made whipped cream and maple syrup. He savored a few bites and pushed it away.

"What I need, Genie, is a bit of the medicine from Colton's. It calms the pain."

"It's right here, Papa. Here, let me put some in a cup for you." It reeked. Probably straight whiskey camouflaged in the patent medicine bottle under Dr. Foley's name – well, with maybe a bit of heroin. Ordinarily, a ruckus would be raised at the first sniff of it, but it came from Colton's apothecary shop, and it did ease the pain, and the doctor said.

In just a few minutes, Mr. Fuller felt better, tasted more of the bread pudding, and then said quietly, "Eugenia, we need to talk." When he used her full name, she knew he was serious.

"Genie, keep the farm as long as you can. Josiah and Amos will work it, and they won't cheat you out of the land. The land is everything. Remember, foes can take your money and ruin your name; they can't take your land unless you let them. When you move your mother to town, rent the farm. You can't take care of it – neither can Em or Char and her family. If Josiah or Amos's families want to rent it, then give them first pick. Rent it for a token and make your money off a percentage of the crops and lumber. Otherwise, there are plenty more people interested. I've showed you how to take care of the books and Abraham will help you, I know.

"Abraham. What are you going to do, Genie?"

"I don't know, Papa. I want to go to California. He doesn't. I want to keep teaching. He says no. I detest politics. It delights him. We've been friends most of our lives. I could never choose anyone else. He says the same."

"A team of horses pulls together, Genie. They move in unison. You're both thoroughbreds racing your own track, it seems. Whatever you decide will be for the best. You three girls are jewels in my life, and you each have your own brilliance. You will make the world a better place. I could use a little more medicine."

Eugenia uncapped the bottle and, using his special silver teaspoon, poured two helpings into the weathered cup.

The Fuller Cemetery on the Homestead

The Board of Education in Galesburg, Illinois

The Board of Education of Galesburg School District was organized on June 11, 1861. Except for the records as outlined in Steele's <u>Galesburg Public Schools</u> (1911), School Board files are missing for the first two years, and there are no preserved files of any newspapers published in Galesburg from 1860-1870, unless they are stacked in someone's attic. School buildings were temporary, organization was loose, and salaries were meager. The "Principal of the Graded Schools" was allocated seven hundred dollars for the year, and all other teachers were paid by the week. The "lady teachers" at the high school were paid at six dollars per week, and all other teachers received five dollars per week.

Among the names of teachers listed on the roll in 1862 was Miss Mary Allen West who was assigned a lower south room in the Colton Building (L Grammar School). By September 1863, a separate school for colored children was opened, and Miss Mary Allen West was the teacher who was appointed at a salary of six dollars per week. This is the same Mary Allen West who lived to achieve a state and national reputation as an educator and temperance worker and who served as an early master educator role model for Eugenia Fuller.

Since the School Board members functioned as employers and administrators, it was common for parents and teachers to take their requests and complaints to the Board. Some matters seemed to be trivial but needed answers or mediation. For instance, a teacher needed approval for a day's leave of absence. Two other teachers who occupied the same room needed help because they could not come to an agreement as to the way the desks should be arranged, and they asked the Board to make a decision. The Board adopted a resolution that essentially appointed a committee to make decisions, thus alleviating pressure on board members.

There were extensive disagreements over the length of the lunch hours. It was made at first for a half hour; then it was changed to an hour. By the following month, the lunch time was increased to an hour and a half. Some parents disliked teachers who used strong corporal punishment, and they complained to the Board about mistreatment of their children. Some wanted their relatives to be assigned as teachers rather than the relatives of their neighbors. Truancy, plain lack of attendance, and tardiness all comprised serious problems. A rule was made that falsely signed excuses could result in expulsion from school. These matters, largely relegated to principals of the future, were frequent considerations for members of the School Board and caused anxious talk and controversy from one meeting to another.

Sighs of relief and a feeling that burdens had rolled away occurred when some of the responsibility for decision-making was transferred to Mr. J. B. Roberts, a teacher of High School classes who was identified as the principal-teacher, then the principal, later the Principal-Superintendent, and finally the Superintendent. When he was re-elected for employment in 1866, the term Superintendent of City Schools was used as his title.

The title of High School Principal evolved in much the same way, and at the time when Eugenia Fuller was assigned to teach High School classes, the principal was Mrs. Mary E. Gettemy. There had been reluctance in appointing women to the principalships, and Mr. Steele presents an ironic picture of the dilemma that confronted Board members around 1870.

> There was a strong sentiment from the very first that the head of the Grammar School should be a man, as was the Principal of the High School. When the schools were organized, the grammar department was placed in the Colton Building and A. E. Blunt was made Principal. When Mr. Blunt resigned, in January 1863, the Board, not being able to get a man for the vacancy thus caused, after much hesitation made Mrs. R. K. Colby head of the department for the remainder of the school year. Mr. Edward H. Curtis was elected Principal for the next year, with Mrs. Colby as his assistant. This action of the Board

caused the resignation of Mrs. Colby and, apparently, that of two or three other teachers. Mr. Curtis held the position but one year, and from that date, the place has been held by a woman. When Edward Hayes resigned as Principal of the High School in 1869, that position was also filled by a woman and continued to be so filled for twenty-six years. When the Fourth Ward School was opened in January 1870, Miss Wheelock was made the Principal, but three years later when the Fifth Ward School was opened, Mr. Patrick Talent was placed at its head. At the close of this period there were three men connected with the schools: J. B. Roberts, Superintendent of Schools, Patrick Talent, Principal of the Fifth Ward School, and LeRoy S. Bates, a teacher in one of the grades in the High School building.

For Eugenia, 1877 was a banner year. She graduated from Lombard College, entered the program for a master's degree and was soon offered a teaching position and principalship at the Seventh Ward School. The salary was $450.00, and she had the responsibilities (which by this time had been well formulated) for a principal of the Grammar School. She was now able to earn her way. She roomed at the Browning mansion on Kellogg Street, conferred with her sisters who were already teaching, and visited often with her parents either at the farm or when they came to lectures at Lombard or Knox or made their ritual trips to town for supplies and to catch up on the news. Her fiancé, Abraham Brown, an attorney in town, had taught in Galesburg in the early 1870s and, from time to time, he and Eugenia had vibrant discussions about the policies of the district, the influx of immigrants, the issues about educating the blacks, and politics, in general.

For most of the others in the education ranks that year, the banner was a red flag, and there was open resentment about having the salaries cut ten percent, increased enrollments, higher expectations to maintain, and facilities in an increasing state of disrepair. The next year was worse because salaries were cut another ten percent. The economic picture was bleak.

On the other hand, some exciting events took place and honors were bestowed upon worthy graduates and long serving Board members. A school beautification was emphasized in March of 1879, and trees were planted around the buildings. The town began to regain the pride and bustling energy that had been dormant or depressed during the past few years. Part of the previous disenchantment may have stemmed from the resignation of Superintendent Brooks after a twelve-year tenure for a similar position in a larger area, and the subsequent appointment of Superintendent Andrews in 1874-75. There was a gradual transfer of administrative duties away from the Board and to the Superintendent who became known for his emphasis on keeping accurate records, being punctual, and maintaining a clear practical course of study in all classes. By 1879, it was noted that school attendance had improved noticeably, and that discipline seemed to be more in control. By the time Superintendent Andrews left the system in 1885 to take a position in Oakland, California, teachers and principals wrote letters of resolution that praised his work and showed admiration for him as a person.

In 1882, Eugenia became "the other teacher" at the High School under the leadership of Mrs. Mary E. Gettemy, the Principal, and with the good will and confidence of Superintendent Andrews. Members of the Board had known her family for many years and spoke on her behalf. Miss Fuller knew that Mr. Andrews was strong in his opinions about organization, about keeping the students up to grade level and not permitting large gaps in their learning patterns and course content, all of which she assiduously ascribed. She found that Mrs. Gettemy had a special style which enabled her to get tasks accomplished quickly and without much fanfare, and a way of involving students – even reluctant ones – and endearing them to her forever.

The High School was the first building to obtain city water for drinking purposes, and led the way with providing a fire escape. Telephones were installed, not by directive of the Board, but by the fire and police departments and by Order of the City Council for civic purposes. By 1880, the enrollment at the High School was 119, and the course of study had been revised.

> In this period the High School was generally regarded as an institution whose purpose was to prepare its students for college. Superintendent Andrews recommended in his annual report for 1880 that the course be extended to four years, and that Greek be introduced so that students might be thoroughly prepared for the Freshman class in the classified course of the colleges. (Steele, p.97)

At the same time, Steele reported that Superintendent Andrews recommended that Bookkeeping be made a part of the curriculum. In 1884, the third printed course of study appeared which indicated that continued concern and emphasis was placed on curriculum development.

By 1885, the school facilities were being remodeled and enlarged, and provisions had been made for new buildings to accommodate the additional students as more people came into the area, and as interest in high school education escalated. Even so, Eugenia had become restless in spite of the innovations, including those she herself had introduced into classroom programs that had added to her popularity and zest. Her plans for marriage had not materialized for a number of reasons, yet she could not bring herself to consider anyone but Abe. Her dear father's death more than two years ago stirred deep loneliness and anger because he had left her, and sorrow at seeing his empty chair, not hearing his encouraging voice nor having his needed reassurance caused her to consider what she really wanted from life and what her next move should be. Her father had been a roamer in his early years, and she smiled as she recognized the same trait in herself. Too, Charlotte was in Harvard, Nebraska with her preacher husband and his children, so the family pattern had already been broken twice. Emily and her mother were not surprised when Eugenia announced gingerly but definitely one evening that she planned to move West at the end of the term. Nor were they surprised to hear that she would go to Riverside, California, for letters came frequently from the Western Mecca that described Riverside as paradise on earth. Some of the most respected and wealthy families in Galesburg were selling out and planning new homesteads in the city of sunshine, space, future wealth, and a God given heaven of opportunity. There was one recurring thought and wish that Eugenia kept close to her heart. Maybe – just maybe – she could do in Riverside what Mary Allen West had done in Galesburg. Someday there would be a high school in Riverside and a Principal and a Superintendent. There was fertile ground to break in many ways. Universities would be established. Real estate was to be had for the taking, practically, and surely would become valuable in the future. Already, she had made some wise investments, particularly with the railroads, and Abe had taught her to be familiar with mortgages, loans, and real estate. She could teach and be an independent person at the same time.

It didn't mean that she would be there forever. Several families in Galesburg had homes and businesses in both places. Travel was not that expensive – not with railroad incentives. It was just putting up with the long days and nights of travel. With the convenience of dining and Pullman cars, she could have adventure after adventure and have the best of both worlds. Besides, that would be a perfect way to entice Abraham to travel to California and be converted to the Riverside style. She didn't want to use the word desperate, but she yearned to leave the only area she knew for adventures in the West. Horace Greeley and his peers were right, she thought. She tilted her hat, raised her chin and swished down Kellogg Street with dramatic effect. Anyone watching her would have declared that the lady had a bee in her bonnet.

CHURCHILL SCHOOL.
North Hall of Second Floor was the High School. 1867-1888.

Churchill School
where Galesburg High School classes were conducted

Broken Engagement

"There's no use for us to continue. We've been over our differences and opinions dozens of times, and Genie, you just won't listen to reason. You know there's no way I'd **ever** consent to teach those black kids and I don't want you to be involved either. Something's happening to our country, and it's not good."

"Abe, the times are changing. The war is over and we have to put aside..."

"Put aside? Why should **we** be the ones to 'put aside?' I know what you're going to say, and I emphatically say **no**. I quit teaching and went into law when the black tykes came to school, as you know, because I'd never, never touch or teach black kids. And I'm determined to win the Senate seat and make sure we pass laws to keep the level of education up and people separated according to their kind."

"But, Abe, education isn't suffering. I see teachers coming to school early every day so that they can help eager children who are so new to the program. Emily and I are working with parents on the weekends. Every parent I've encountered is excited about their children getting an education. Just because I work with them is no reason to reject me, is it Abe?"

"You're different now. I remember the good times when we planned a life together, to have children, to join our farms, and have a house in town – but then you start getting ideas and going to meetings, and you've become so independent and strong and outspoken that – and that's not a woman's place! Lots of people are talking about it. I'm not the only one!"

"Well, Abraham, tell me. What is a woman's place?"

"Get the steel out of your voice, Genie. That won't work on me. You're beautiful. You're charming. You're persuasive, but not with me.

You're over educated. You have values I never heard of in a beautiful woman. It's the education that's done it and those damn abolitionists."

"And you're including my parents and sisters, Abe, as well as members of your own family."

"I don't know about anything any more. I just know that we can't go on like this."

"Then I think we must part while we are still friends." Eugenia moved from her chair and reached out her hand. "You know that you are my life's blood. You know I love you more than life itself, and we cannot let bitterness destroy what we have had. Goodbye, Abraham. Be always well and remember that I shall be your friend forever. Forever, Abe." Her throat tightened and the last words were caught in the grip.

Abe stood and took both her hands into his. He gently caressed her finger wearing his ring. "Oh, my God, Genie. Oh, my dear, this can't be happening. In a hoarse, tear-laced voice, he told her of his love for her and whispered. "Please wear the ring on any finger you want, but wear it and remember me. You will always be my beloved." He picked up his hat, bowed, and closed the door quietly as he left without a backward look.

Eugenia stood there in front of the closed door. She didn't – couldn't – move for a time. Then she went from the guest sitting room section of her classroom to her desk. She sat there a very long time – numb with hot shame and prickles running through her body. If Abraham rejected her – the love of her life – how could anyone else think well of her. Tears, more tears, more tears. She couldn't stop them. As usual when she faced crises, she tried to lecture herself aloud. No words would come from her constricted throat, but sobs escaped in a gulping, erratic pattern. She choked and the breath inside her could not come out. The soggy handkerchief was useless and the tears continued to fall on her blouse and the papers on the desk. The office, indeed the whole school, was empty except perhaps for the janitor. She was thankful for that. The late afternoon sun dimmed, and still she sat and agonized over the sudden change in her life. He might change his mind and offer to continue. It would never be the same. How could she go on with someone who lost respect for her and had such harsh views of others? How could she go on facing people who were treating her civilly to her face and making negative retorts to others. Abraham wouldn't have told her that others were gossiping about her were it not true.

The numbness and burning and the terrible rushes of shame did not subside. Hot as she was, goosebumps appeared on her arms, and the golden red hairs stood erect. She wanted to scream, scream and yell. Her head was splitting and only by gripping the desk with both hands, she kept herself upright. Eugenia sat at her desk until nearly dark. Then she straightened the papers, put on her hat, and looked in the mirror near the door. She had a plan, and now all she needed was the courage to carry it out. She lightly touched the framed quotation by the door as she left and decided to do just that.

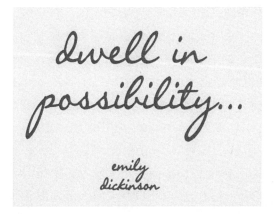

Eugenia turned right at the corner of the next block and nearly ran into Mrs. Nussam who was hurrying home from her day job herself. "Oh, Miss Fuller, excuse me! Even with the new street lamps and the light of the full moon, I didn't see you. I'm so sorry!"

"My dear Mrs. Nussam, do not apologize. The fault is mine. My thoughts were elsewhere. I wasn't paying attention."

"Now Miss Fuller! Not paying attention? Don't let your charges hear you say that. My lips are sealed!

"Miss Fuller? Miss Fuller? Are you all right? You work much too hard. You will burn yourself out. I don't mean to intrude, but you don't sound like yourself tonight. It's late. Go home, my dear, and get some rest."

"Oh, yes, Mrs. Nussam, I am on my way. And you, too, must get some rest. Please hug your little ones for me. And I must tell you that your son, Paul, is doing you and Mr. Nussam proud. Only yesterday, Mrs. Gettemy told me how well he is doing with his recitations and public speaking." She put her hand on Mrs. Nussam's arm. "Goodnight."

"God Bless you, Miss Fuller. God bless you and keep you well."

Eugenia opened the door to Em's wail. "Genie, where in the world have you been? I was about to go looking for you. Supper's cold, but it's still on the table. I fed the cats, and now I'm going to bed since I know you're all right."

"Em, stay. Stay for a bit. I'm not all right."

"What's happened? Oh, my God, look at your face. It's swollen. You've been crying."

"Yes."

"What happened at school?"

"Abraham came to see me after school today. In a matter of minutes, life as I know it – knew it – is gone." Silence. Emily waited.

More silence. Emily leaned closer and barely whispered, "And?"

"He's embarrassed, and he won't accept or support my views on just about anything. He wants me to reflect his. You know that I can't. The political life is not for me."

Emily made tea. She and Genie sat at the kitchen table and tried to sort out feelings as they nibbled on sumptuous cheesecake – though barely tasting it – and raised their cups from time to time. When they retired, Eugenia fell asleep almost immediately. It was Emily who lay awake, already grieving for the sister who went away. She might be sleeping in the next room, but it was clear. Eugenia was on her way to a future without her.

Two More Days
1886

The outfit hung on the open door of her bedroom. It was brown, beige, and had a touch of yellow. Those were the best colors to wear on the smoky train, she had decided. She might have to wear it for days, and she wanted to look presentable when she stepped off the train and made her way to her Riverside destination. Despite the current styles, she had designed and sewn a simple skirt, a jacket, and two cotton shirts, one with a ruffled neckline and one with an almost risqué v-neckline. Both buttoned down the front. The big problem was the petticoats she was expected to wear. She decided that she would only wear two on the train and put on the others as she neared her destination. After all, she would be sitting most of the time. Her brown leather shoes were on the floor by the dresser. The stylish boot-shoes had elegant high heels and buttoned above her ankles. She had worn them twice to break them in, and before that, she had put them in bed beside her so she could admire the style and enjoy the smell of new shoes before she went to sleep. On the packed trunk near the window, she had laid out a beige hat, a yellow floral scarf, and a pair of gloves that buttoned at the wrist. Two days from now, she would board the train at ten o'clock in the morning and begin an adventure.

In the butterfly moments when she needed courage, she cheered herself with Goethe's mantra: "Rest not! Life is sweeping by; Go and dare before you die. Something mighty and sublime, Leave behind to conquer time."

Even so, Eugenia had not been sleeping well. Every part of her throbbed and her tummy was on a roller coaster, jumping up and down and then sliding with a bit of a shiver, while her throat was nearly swollen shut with excitement and gaspy breathing. She was going to California – going in two days – and could still hardly believe it in spite of her sewing and shopping and packing for the last two months. She knew she would be safe. Still, the furthest she had been away from home was to Chicago and her sister's home in Nebraska. Now, in her late twenties, she was going by train from Galesburg, Illinois to Riverside, California, more than two thousand miles away. Lord have mercy.

As she dressed and went downstairs to greet Emily, she marveled about how very easy it had been to be hired as a teacher. Friends who had left Galesburg and established themselves in Riverside had spoken on her behalf to the Board and the matter was settled when Mr. Holmes, Mr. Wilbur, and Mr. Allen acted on the recommendation. Just like that. The O. T. and A. P. Johnson families had offered her board and room, and so she would still be living with Galesburgers, surrounded by longtime neighbors from the North Henderson area, and only miles from several college friends from Lombard who had preceded her exodus. All that was left to do was to say goodbyes, promise to come home to visit – or maybe even come back to live soon – and this was the hardest part. She would have lunch with Abraham today, and the very thought of parting from him lurched her into despair. Perhaps he would soon come to California, too. That possibility made it bearable, but she knew how important being an Illinois State Senator meant to him, so her feelings went back and forth from ecstasy to agony.

Emily was banging pots and pans. That meant she was more frustrated than usual. Anytime Emily got upset, she told the world by the way she handled kitchen utensils. "Oh, my good Lord, Em, settle your wits!"

"Why, why, why? Why should I? You want me to keep my feelings inside and go crazy? Come on, now. There's fresh strawberry jam to go with your muffins. Eat up, and tell me again about your new job," she said as she shed her apron and pulled her chair up to the table, too. "Come on, and tell me this jam is delicious."

"I've told you all I know, Em. The district is small, not as big as Galesburg. What I teach depends upon the ages of the students. Of course, I want to teach algebra, geometry, and trigonometry, but I may end up teaching multiplication facts and fractions. It could be that I'll have all ages and all subjects. I just don't know. But isn't it exciting?"

"You promised to write often. Keep your promise, Genie."

"I will. I promise. I'll write you every week once I get settled. And you, too. Promise to tell me everything that happens in town and North Henderson. And promise to apprise me about our mother's progress. I think she'll do much better now that she's living here in town with Uncle Nick."

"Promises, promises. Yes, you know I will. I'll write all the news and all the gossip. Especially the gossip."

"And you'll come visit when school is out in the spring."

"I think I will! Genie, you always put me back into a good mood. You always do. Don't forget; we're driving the carriage to the homestead this afternoon so we can store the rest of Mama and Papa's treasures in the summer kitchen for safekeeping. Let's stay overnight. It will be our last opportunity before the renters show up to sign the lease tomorrow."

The plans were made and the hours passed. Now there would be just one more day before getting on the train.

Riverside, California

Copy of a vintage greeting card

On to California

Eugenia had characteristics of her legendary cousin Margaret Fuller in that she had arranged to go traveling alone and would not be intimidated or manipulated by others who disapproved of a young woman being confronted with probable dangers. Several families setting out for Riverside at about the same time had offered to escort her or to have her supervise their children on the trip for a sizable fee, but she declined by explaining how she had longed for so many years to be a pioneer and experience what it must have been like for those who set the pattern for exploring unknown territory. No one argued. People seldom confronted Miss Eugenia Fuller.

Cold rain – almost sheets of icy sleet – helped her bid goodbye to the only home and people she had ever known and loved. The unusual chill penetrated and seemed to immobilize her throat and lay a heaviness in her chest. She had not known it would be so difficult to leave one area and go to another to further her own career. She kept telling herself, "It isn't final. It isn't final." Deep down, she knew that she was closing a door to a significant part of her life. As a little child, she had heard people quoting President Lincoln as saying, "When you close one door, my child, another one opens," and for days she had gone through the house closing a door to see if another one would open and learned that she had to open the doors herself. She lectured herself about the need for being calm and brave and as the massive train door clanged shut, she raised her head high and was seen by those about her as a lady of courage, wisdom, and economic means who was impatient for the train to move on.

The route had been figured out with care. The first lap would be to take the Q to Chicago. Then from Chicago, there would be the long, long trek to Los Angeles with a few stops along the way at Harvey Houses. That was something new added to this line. Now she didn't have to worry about wearing the same soiled clothes over and over and arriving in a disheveled condition. The train would stop periodically, and then she could have the comforts of home according to the brochure that the conductor handed to each passenger. It far surpassed the one that Silvanus Ferris brought back after visiting Riverside. Progress seemingly occurred with every trip. There was an additional fee for this service and not every itinerary offered it because it delayed the estimated time of arrival. From Los Angeles, she would go to Colton and then take a Glenwood Hotel coach to Riverside. 'Count on a week or more,' she'd been told.

It was not an easy trip. When windows were open, the wind was too strong and pulled ashes and mosquitoes and flies inside. The mesh on the windows helped only a little. When the windows were closed, body smells of unwashed travelers sickened her. So did the loud talk of some of the uncouth men. Flasks were passed around and manners worsened even though the porters tried to soften the situation. It didn't work because the porters were black and received blunt, castigating remarks for their efforts. Fortunately, the dining car had rules for deportment, and fortunately, a number of families were on board to discourage unruly behavior. One young man, on a dare, approached Eugenia for conversation, but he retreated with her curt statement and icy glare. "Chiggers, how kin a woman that purty set you back to a kid?" His goaders laughed and said, "We told you so. Ya can't mess with schoolmarms and dimes to pennies, that's what she is. She sure is a looker, though."

Eugenia kept a careful log of the weather – especially the extreme temperatures, the lightning storms, and the steamy rains – and jotted bits of conversations so that she could insert them in a book some day or at least use the anecdotes in her classes or in letters back home. When she could get a little privacy, she looked at her financial ledger, reviewed poetry she had written recently, and read the Overland Monthly. She did not want to nap off and miss anything on this exciting trip.

While planning her move to Riverside, Eugenia had gathered information in a few blank booklets about how Riverside came to be, the important people who settled the community, the present citizens, and the plans for progress. She pulled one from her satchel and reviewed the notes she had jotted down over the last couple of years about Riverside. It was both ironic and a comfort to realize the similarities in the settlements of Galesburg and Riverside.

There was 'the good doctor,' James P. Greves, who along with John W. North had a great idea of forming a colony in California that would be utopian – Oneida like, and it would be planned, invited, prosperous, and committed from the start. Men of means and talents were targeted, but those who had less were still eligible with a percentage down and written contracts plus a willingness to learn skills and be an integral part of the colony. Education facilities were of top priority, so building schools and libraries were of the utmost importance and required the support of potential colonists. Not following the prescribed plans would invalidate the rights to be a member of the group.

Certainly, if all the stories she had heard were true, the two men had invested, earned money, lost money, and had been nearly run out of town together. They were an enigmatic pair and learned to work together through successes and failures. Eugenia was amazed that they were still acting like young entrepreneurs at their advanced ages. Most men would be yearning for front porch comfort and someone to listen to their adventures – not traveling up, down, and across the country for new beginnings.

The two men were exceptional in other ways. Dr. Greves graduated from the best medical school in the country at the time – College of Physicians and Surgeons of the Western District of New York. He first practiced in Marshall, Michigan, the community that sponsored the Anti-Slavery Society, and he became an activist. His life changed with the death of his daughter. His health declined, he left his Presbyterian faith for Spiritualism, and he separated from his wife and two sons. He dedicated himself to working for a time in Port Royal of the Sea Islands off the coast of South Carolina, and his health declined again. He gave up medicine.

Mr. John Wesley North was an abolitionist, too. He was appointed Surveyor General of the silver-rich Nevada Territory by President Lincoln with the hope that in such an isolated area North could perhaps keep Nevada Territory loyal to the Union and perhaps bring Nevada into the Union as a Republican State. Maybe – just maybe – North's vociferous abolitionist activism would be less noticeable to the public in the East and smooth the waters as Mr. Lincoln assumed the Presidency. That's where Mr. North met Dr. Greves. The two men found they had common interests and they left Nevada as a team to establish an Oneida-like settlement in Knoxville, Tennessee. They were considered outsiders and troublemakers, consequently nearly went broke, and were run out of town for abolitionist activities. Mr. North's reputation for previously founding the Northfield, Minnesota community had been sound, so based on that history, he and Dr. Greves decided to move on and commit to a new settlement – this time in California in 1870.

Additional influential names that Eugenia would need to know about were A. C. Twogood, Dr. K. D. Shugart, S. C. Evans, E. G. Brown, Dr. Eastman, Thomas W. Cover, D. C. Twogood, L. D. Waite, T. J. Wood, J. W. Linville, David Meacham, S. G. Lovell, Dick Reeves, and Hon. C. N. Felton. Comments noted after these names in her booklet were brief, but pointed out how important these men were in getting Riverside settled so that it became Paradise on Earth. Most of the families were still active in the community, and there would certainly be children or grandchildren of these families for her to teach.

Eugenia was dedicated to doing her homework. She had a copy of the brochure that Dr. Greves and Mr. North sent out to possible subscribers to the new settlement. It was idealistic and firm in the expectations for applicants. She had been surprised to learn that Riverside was the colony's second name. The first one was Jurupa and she must remember to pronounce the J like an H. Many of the place names, she'd been told, were

Spanish and learning Spanish would be additional homework. She would get to meet peaceful Cahuilla Indians. They had been workers for the new colony and had their own village on the slope of a mountain in town. The Serranos were nearby, too.

Mr. North and Dr. Greves were still living, and Eugenia determined to meet both of them. Dr. Greves still lived in Riverside and was revered. He had been the postmaster for years and participated in the town's activities, she'd been told. She would meet him soon with the help of a Galesburg friend. Mr. North was a different story. He had moved about and currently was living near an inland town called Fresno. She wanted to ask him what it was like to be a teacher at the age of fifteen, what kinds of programs that Cazenovia Seminary and Wesleyan University offered in the early part of the century, and why he chose to be a lawyer in so many settings. He and Abraham would have interests in common since both were so active in politics. Abraham, though, had never voiced a desire to be a state governor or a Justice on a state Supreme Court, and he had never been sued by his compatriots. It was said that legal entanglements at one point caused Mr. North's health to decline, but he persevered. Yes, she wanted to meet them both and compare their pursuits to the grand adventures of those who had successfully founded the settlement of Galesburg in the 1830s. The similar histories were fascinating, and now she was part of them.

She closed the booklet. There was so much to learn and remember. Her eyes were dry and she was weary, mostly from the rhythm of the wheels on the track and pejorative comments that were impossible to ignore. Tomorrow, she would review all her notes again and practice pronouncing the names – of citizens and of the Spanish terms that had been supplied to her.

Her second booklet would cue her in on other citizens: the Tibbets family that started the citrus industry with the planting of Eliza's orange trees, the Gage family that, along with others, harnessed the waterways, the educators in the towns of Riverside, San Bernardino, and Redlands, and of course all kinds of information about San Bernardino County and the current arguments for creating a new county to be called Riverside. Some of the stories weren't pretty, but she needed to know about the community's reaction to the Chinese culture in Riverside, the railroad fights in Southern California, the feuds over the use of water, behavior in the rowdy West, including the hanging tree in Holcomb Valley and other lore, and the laws that had been passed to keep Riverside pristine in comparison to San Bernardino.

Paradise on Earth

Nothing Eugenia had heard from Galesburgers returning home after a visit to Riverside, no brochure that she had held in her hands as she yearned to see Riverside for herself came close to her vision as the Glenwood coach traveled across the countryside from Colton, then through the famous downtown Riverside and on to Mr. Miller's hotel. It occurred to her that maybe she was Alice and had fallen down the rabbit hole into a delicious wonderland dream that surpassed Alice's visit to the Queen's garden. Unbelievable beauty was everywhere. First, the sky was so beautiful. It reminded her of times she and her mom lay on the grassy knoll and found cloud pictures, except she thought she could actually touch these beauties. She basked in the clear air and made remarks to herself about being able to see mountains far away. Then there were the magnificent colors! Only the word magnificent would do, and she smiled as she remembered her father adding that word to her vocabulary so many years ago. Flowers and vines and trees she had never seen before really did make her feel that she was in a paradise and she wondered if this is what heaven would be like. "Or maybe this is heaven," she said softly to herself.

Enough. The coach pulled up to the entrance and she saw her Galesburg friends waiting and waving to her. "I am so excited by all this loveliness," she said out loud to herself. "Please God, please don't let me embarrass myself by being overcome." All she saw was beauty, beauty that surpassed the growing pains of any community in its infancy. By afternoon, after enjoying refreshments at Mr. Miller's inn and traveling in an elegant carriage on up to the Johnson home on Arlington Avenue, she had time to examine the home where she would board, rest a bit, and then ready herself for a lawn party where her Galesburger hosts would proudly introduce

Riverside's new school teacher to her new home and the many guests. In the cooling hours of the early evening, Eugenia marveled at the loveliness of the large, delicate rose petals, of the tall, sturdy palm trees, of gently fluttering eucalyptus leaves, of fascinating welcoming citizens and their joy of living in Paradise on Earth. It was true. Being here was joyful. She knew in her heart that she was home.

In the months that followed, when some newcomers complained about the unpaved streets, sloshing rains that overflowed the usually dry Santa Ana River and made getting to San Bernardino, the County Seat, nearly impossible, desert heat that seared the skin with just normal exposure during the summer, and blackened skies caused by smudge pots in the winter, Eugenia did little more than wrinkle her nose. After all, she and many of her fellow citizens were from Galesburg and were used to real concerns – rapidly changing temperatures, thunderstorms, tornadoes, high humidity, five-foot snowdrifts, and blackened skies from train belches. Oh, no. Riverside really was Paradise.

**O. T. Johnson House
on Arlington Avenue
(later the May Henry House)**

Early Riverside
Pictures courtesy of Tom Patterson's collection

Learning is a Joy Forever
October 1886

What excitement! What fervor! What pioneering pride! On whose part? Everyone's. Eugenie, her students, the School Board, the parents, the community. Her seven students were at different levels with different needs and different aims. Word got around fast about Miss Fuller's competence and buoyant personality that energized her students. She met compliments and smiles and respect and had to lecture herself in front of the mirror each morning about not letting all the adulation go to her head. Her father's words hung in the air and underscored her thoughts. "Remember, Genie," she could hear him say, "every day is a new opportunity to do your best. It's a test of your character. You may earn a reputation, and it may be good. I'm sure it will be for you. That's what other people think of you. More important, what do you think of you? How you behave and what you do is your character. Don't ever smudge that."

"It's your greatest treasure," Eugenie added aloud, mimicking her father's words. "Keep your head and be yourself, no matter what others think of you."

"Yes, Papa. I'll remember." On this particular morning, she arranged her hat, tilted it a bit and smiled at her reflection. "I'll remember, Papa, but I must tell you, everyone smiles and encourages me. It's so very pleasant."

Eugenie walked from the Johnson home to the Arlington School on Sierra and Palm Avenue in just a few minutes because she was so eager to get there and be prepared and in place before her students arrived. Besides, she wanted them to know that punctuality was an absolutely necessary trait she wanted to instill.

When they arrived, she showed interest in each one, remarked on their promptness, and asked about their parents. Camaraderie developed to a point, and then she was all business. The students struggled, but didn't complain. It took only one session to learn that Miss Fuller didn't accept excuses or professed inadequacy. Each morning was filled with arduous work on mathematics, rhetoric, and both physical and natural sciences before a twenty-minute recess to relax and socialize. The noon hour could be used to go home for lunch, go to the drug store for a soda, or sit somewhere behind the school to eat in solitude or as a group. By 1:00, the students were back at their study tables, inspired to tackle history, geography, and government. Before dismissal at 4:00, there was a thirty-minute period for questions. If the students didn't have them, Miss Fuller did. Years later, the former classmates declared the question period was the most valuable part of the program. Miss Fuller encouraged provocative thought and lauded direct answers without "beating around the bush." Nearly always, an open-ended question from Miss Fuller was pondered on the way home and was part of the dinner table discussion in the evening. Often the questions were repeated at the bank when customers were in a queue, or at the market when women carried on gossip of the day while checking the firmness of tomatoes. On several occasions, Miss Fuller's questions were featured as sermon topics on Sunday mornings. "Last Tuesday, Miss Fuller, our esteemed educator from back East, elicited responses from her students with the following question: 'If someone needed your help, but was too proud to ask, and if you knew that offering help would severely impinge on your own resources, and that nobody would know of your inner thoughts about the matter, honestly now, what would you do?' Her follow-up question was 'Why?' Those of us in this great community of Riverside, where special needs of all sorts occur, will do well to focus on these soul-searching questions this morning as we gather in the Lord's house."

In one instance, Eugenie Fuller sat quietly in a pew near the back of the United Presbyterian Church and waited for someone's response. Her eyes sparkled and sunshine lit her face when one of her students stood up and articulated in a full voice and with thoughtful insight. "As Papa would say, his character speaks well of him and his family," she thought to herself. "He's willing to take a public stand."

In no time at all, the '86-87 term ended. Eugenie had never been so happy, so fulfilled, so eager for her classes to start again at Magnolia and Palm Avenues in Riverside's Sunnyside/Arlington District.

Her enthusiasm was contagious. Her students counted the days, too, and reminded her of the count when they met her on the street or at church. "That," she told them in each instance, "is the sincerest compliment my ears have ever heard."

Teachers' Institute at Riverside
April 18-22, 1887

A joint Teachers' Institute for San Diego and San Bernardino Counties was scheduled for five days in Riverside, beginning April 18, 1887. As hosts, Eugenie (now with an ie) and Professor Twining, the San Bernardino County Teacher-Principal, had major roles in planning and implementing the event. The students would not be penalized by losing class time because the Institute was to be held during Easter Vacation. Educators from both large counties were eager (and virtually required) to attend. (Riverside was not a county at the time.)

"The place chosen for the meeting was peculiarly appropriate for the purpose. Riverside, the superb, the center of California orange growing, was a sea of green trees, whose greenness was intensified by the millions of bright blossoms exhaling their fragrance on every hand. Brilliant roses, pure orange flowers, verbenas, carnations, pansies, marguerites, geraniums, flaming pomegranates, apple, peach, pear, plum, and a hundred other flowers showed their faces in riotous luxuriance along the streets, in the door yards, gardens, and orchards.

"And the drive down Magnolia Avenue, past mile after mile, and mile after mile of trim hedges, under the shade of graceful pepper and stately eucalyptus, with glimpses of blue mountains appearing and disappearing between the trees, with the soft breeze fanning the cheek, with the exquisite perfume of orange groves floating in every breath – it was a fairy land to the tired teachers, after a year's struggle with the problems of education in the school houses of the desert, the mountain, the plain, the sea coast, the valley." (Edward Hyatt, The Pacific Educational Journal, page 250.)

Mr. Henry C. Brooke from San Bernardino and Mr. Rufus D. Butler from San Diego County were the respected Superintendents who gave the opening remarks. Mr. Brooke had been credited with much of the Institute's success in previous years due to his careful decisions and his courteous bearing to everyone. Mr. Butler was known as a scholar who possessed the rare faculty of always saying the right thing in the right place and of stopping when he had said it. Mr. Hoitt, the California State Superintendent of Public Instruction, seemed to be hugely popular with everyone. He was described as a teacher in every sense of the word – earnest, fearless, outspoken in defense of the right, wise, and practical in dealing with the public – indeed, the man of the hour and the key speaker.

After the opening exercises, discussions of the new State Series of Textbooks and the Temporary Classifications of a Public School monopolized the hours. Class leaders on the second day of the Institute were Misses Rose Hardenberg, **Eugenie Fuller**, F. A. Brown, Cora Lamb, A. T. Starbird, Mrs. Curtis, and Messrs. C. H. Woods, N. A. Richardson and **N. C. Twining**. They led workshops in Primary Reading, Primary Arithmetic, Algebra, Philosophy, Sentential Analysis, and English Literature. The third and fourth days noted other leaders who spoke on subjects of Language, Writing, Drawing, Music, Natural History, Common School Essentials, Grammar Grade Arithmetic, Grammar, Geography, and History. There was no slowdown in the scheduled events. Composition, Mental Arithmetic, and Orthoepy were also discussed for a block of time.

"The entire proceedings were enlivened and made attractive by songs, by violin, piano, organ, and choir music, by recitations, by banks of roses, garlands of orange flowers, wreaths of myrtles, and other blooms ad infinitum; all furnished by the good people of Riverside." (Hyatt, page 251)

Edward Hyatt noted in his minutes that two night sessions were held – one was a lecture delivered by Superintendent Hoitt. A reception was given by the Hotel Glenwood one evening, and a ball was given by the Knights of Pythias on Thursday evening, to which the teachers were invited.

To summarize all the activities, the Riverside Daily Press reported the proceedings in full, and presented every participant with a copy each day. Passing resolutions and singing 'Home, Sweet Home' concluded the activities. By Monday, everyone was back to their assignments, filled with inspiration and already looking forward to next year's Institute. Eugenie Fuller and N. C. Twining congratulated each other on the successful program each time they saw each other for months afterwards.

Good Times

She hadn't a care in the world. On this sunny, breezy Saturday morning, Eugenia was almost skipping down unpaved Magnolia Avenue, and her golden-red hair, loosened from the pompadour pins, bobbed up and down on her shoulders as she moved. She stooped to pick a flower along the roadway and blew gently on its petals and just kept walking that special cadence of hers which caused even cotton petticoats to swish and hum beneath her yellow skirt. A catchy tune crept into her mind, and she began to whistle just as she used to do as a child when she boosted her courage on the long walks to school. She looked behind her just as she used to do and saw a carriage coming. No fear. It was a parishioner who offered her a lift. Eugenie really wanted to keep walking, but to be polite and friendly, she grasped the holding pole, lifted her skirt enough to be able to make the two steps up and swung herself in place on the leather seat. She was joyous and kept up a steady run of conversation as the carriage swung onto the grounds of the United Magnolia Presbyterian Church where the Christian Endeavor Society youth group was to meet for the day's programs and festivities.

Eugenie had planned it all. Back home in Galesburg, her religious zeal had been nominal, and even her family members commented on her skepticism and lack of enthusiasm for practicing religious traditions. Here, though, she had such a feeling of freedom and euphoria that she soon abandoned her critiques and threw herself wholeheartedly into the Lord's work by writing and producing plays, establishing a junior choir with popular and patriotic songs, and encouraging memorized recitations for Sunday morning services.

Then there was the fun of sharing box lunches, indulging in ice cream socials, playing I Spy games, and bicycling on the privacy of the church grounds. Planting colorful flower beds, building a five-foot-high rock garden, and enlarging the popular duck pond appealed to the budding naturalists in the group. The once monthly conference on Saturdays brought all the participants together and provided a perfect opportunity for important speakers to inculcate the morals of the day: honesty, loyalty, commitment to reaching goals, and hard work.

On frequent Sunday afternoons, the high school girls' youth group combined with the boys' group, and parents, teachers and other interested adults trekked up Mount Rubidoux where everyone, in awe, enjoyed the beauty of the mountain and views of the gorgeous valley below. There were occasional games of tag and hide and seek around the boulders. The vigorous climb made the afternoon picnics a joyous necessity, and a special spirituality pervaded the suddenly reverent group when fifteen minutes of silence were mandated so that each person could think his own thoughts. Years later, grownups would recall those events as the Easter sunrise services were established on the Mount and realize that they had pioneered the tradition with what they called Sunday Treks up the Mountain.

Overburdened parents often asked Miss Fuller where in the world she found the energy to work with high school students during the school week and then devote so much time to them and their activities on the weekend. "Work? It's not work for me. I can't explain the passion I have for learning and to get everyone else excited to feel the same. You see, I believe that all the problems of the universe can be solved with knowledge and caring for others. My mother used to say that I have a Must-Fix-It personality. Remember, I lived through the Civil War and its aftermath, and it was horrible. Where was the Golden Rule? Where was justice? Where was caring? Did so many have to die in order for us to learn to live and learn together?

"We have to make sure that nothing like that happens again. And we must all try to fix the world, Pollyannish as that sounds. One of my very favorite teachers emphasized that home and school is where we start, and that's my credo, too." After a while, parents quit asking. They would only get another version of the same story.

A later view of Mount Rubidoux

Tom Hays Comes to Town
Spring of 1890

Eugenie, on her way home after school, stopped at the Blue Tea Room, a small restaurant on Brockton Avenue. She loved the quiet solace with just a hint of background music from the Victrola, the fragrance of goodies reminiscent of home, and the time to visit with others who dropped by for a cup of tea. Not all comers were English, but all liked the idea of tea in the afternoon. The room was abuzz with conversation, and Eugenie joined friends from the Woman's Club who motioned to her. Everyone shifted just a bit so that Eugenie could pull a chair from the next table and slide in as the seventh guest. The tea, a scone with blueberry jam, and dainty sandwiches arrived promptly, and Eugenie listened avidly as she spread soft butter over the hot biscuit. The talk was about money. Eugenie had more than a passing interest in the gossip this time. She, unlike all the others in the group, was single. That meant that she alone was responsible for keeping herself out of the poorhouse. She had done well so far. A frugal nature, a sizable inheritance, a proclivity for math, and an adventuresome investment spirit for new technology gave her the confidence of a wealthy woman. Certainly, the posted salary she earned at the high school did not contribute anything more than gentility and basic comforts, and allowed virtually nothing to set aside for a calamity, infirmity, or old age.

"There's a new man at the bank."

"Ooh, and he's so handsome!"

"How you talk! He's probably married."

"Well, so am I! But I can still look."

"How old is he?"

"My husband said twenty-three."

"And where's he from?"

"He came here from Los Angeles, but he's from back East, Pennsylvania, I heard."

Eugenie edged in, "What's his name?"

"Tom Hays. His name is Tom Hays. It sounds like a stage name. Can't you just hear – and starring Tom Hays?"

The ladies scarcely tasted their food, but the conversation – mostly about Tom and the bank's expansion – was delicious. The party ended suddenly when one of the women looked at her watch and exclaimed, "Oh, my! My husband's home from work and wondering where I am, and..."

"More importantly," said another, "why his dinner is not on the table!"

The other patrons read or talked quietly with each other, but the overheard conversations caused contagious laughter in the tearoom.

Usually Mrs. Bennett or one of her girls quietly picked up the tickets and money laying on the table, but because there had been such involved conversations and laughter, Mrs. Bennett declined to interrupt. It was a pleasure to have guests enjoying themselves. So this time, the ladies presented their tabs as they passed Mrs. Bennett's desk. Eugenie hung back as the others paid their bills and scurried on, all the while promising to see each other soon. They had to get to their families quickly – for that very reason. They had families.

The proprietor hesitated just a moment as she handed back the change. "Miss Fuller, I want to thank you for helping my Michael get glasses. He's doing ever so much better in school, thanks to your kindness."

"You're so very welcome, Mrs. Bennett. I am amazed that he was able to do as well as he did with such poor vision. It was such a welcome discovery when I pointed out a peacock with spread plumage across a field, and he confessed he couldn't see it! Life is full of miracles, Mrs. Bennett. Being able to enhance your son's eyesight is one of them." Eugenie stepped aside for a friend and then waited for her so they could continue on their way together.

Most dinner tables that evening flourished with conversations about the growing banking industry and the fact that an outsider had been hired as cashier. There was concern among some that an unknown person outside the community had been even considered, and most questioned why since there were such able men in town waiting to be promoted to the cashier's job. Because of booming business in housing construction, in citrus production, in railroading, in road building, in making bigger and better canals, in water deals, and in newcomers moving to town, bankers had high prestige second only to the judges. There were constant reminders about the integrity of the financial backers and the safety these trustees promised with other people's money. All were townspeople of long standing, and only a few had been peremptory enough to raise hackles about the governance of the community's activities. All were seen as decent, married, churchgoing men. Their children, for the most part, stayed out of mischief, and the wives were known as good budgeteers of their household accounts. Riversiders were the best promoters of Riverside as an idyllic community. Its residents were of hardy, pioneer, hard working stock whose previous efforts in life had provided the means to travel to California and to set up residency. Pioneer families had paid to join this early colony, and the tradition persisted through the cost of the land and the expectations for those who chose a piece of paradise. As residents tallied more profits, they looked to the banks as a fortress for their wealth.

Still, with all the smooth assurances, there was a gnawing fear that hard earned money could disappear overnight, and some of the residents had bitter memories to prove it. Sure, there were contracts about bankers promising to make deposits good in case of financial disasters, but there was not a single fail-safe provision in all the written words. If the money wasn't there, and the bankers couldn't honor their promises, that was the end of it – even with long drawn out court battles. Eugenie delayed reading the news, along with eating tidbits from her generous slice of apple pie, while she pulled three account books out of compartments in her rolled desktop and consoled herself as she examined the figures again that at least she hadn't put all of her eggs in one basket.

Riverside School Board Discussion and Action
July 11, 1893

"The principal is responsible for knowing where we are, where we are going, and how we intend to get there."

"And how we will know we've gotten there."

"Yes, and we would expect the principal to run the school and to make the day-to-day decisions. Goodness knows not one of us has the time to be involved in the daily issues that are so important to our teachers and citizens – and I don't think any one of us wants to. Right? I can tell by your aside comments and expressions that you agree with me. We will expect the principal to run the school and keep order and keep the parents supportive of our policies. Right? Right."

"The person we choose will need our support and confidence. That person needs to be in contact with us – someone we know and trust – someone who cares about academic excellence –."

"And someone who will stand up to anyone and everyone to defend justice and individual rights."

"And someone to promote a sense of personal responsibility and leadership in each of our high school students."

"Well, then, gentlemen of the Board, let us cease our discussion and deliberations and make her appointment effective immediately."

"Her? You're thinking of Miss Eugenie Fuller, I gather?"

"Of course. You have described her exactly in the expectations you have for the leader of our high school. She is not only the logical choice of those educators that we know and have considered, she is the only choice. We have searched throughout San Bernardino County, San Diego County, and now our newly formed Riverside County, and we've found NO one as qualified."

"Well, Gentlemen – what is your pleasure?"

"Well, I speak for her confirmation on her academic record, but I must mention that she's such a strong-willed woman. Very independent – and perhaps far ahead of her time in many ways. She may be too far ahead for the people of this town."

"For the most part, the community respects her because of the connections she has with educators at the university level and for her own standards which are very high. There are some town leaders, though, who think she does not do what they want. She is not easy to change when her mind is made up."

"That's exactly why we need her. She listens, yes, but makes her decisions herself without leaning towards the saying of the townspeople. She certainly has worked well with most of the teachers and with all of us."
"I agree with you. She's absolutely right for the job and I heartily endorse her appointment.

"It's the perfect time to appoint her inasmuch as this is the first year of creating the Riverside High School District. We've had students graduating since 1890, when we established our program at the Fourteenth Street School, and a large amount of credit goes to her for her dedication - and insistence, I might add."

"Yes, I approve of that. We had seven students in the first graduation - three boys and four girls, and she has opened the doors of both Berkeley and Stanford to them along with the ones who have graduated since. Others have been helpful, too, and let's give Miss Bancroft, Mr. Twining, and Mr. Givens proper credit. In spite of titles on record, Miss Fuller has been the driving force for the success of our high school while it has been under common, local control in our community for years. Now that the State of

California has legally approved high school districts, as of yesterday's date, the official blessing and funding will enable us to expand and do even more. We will be a leading light."

"Another good reason for this designation is that the students will see no interruption in their serious studies. Miss Fuller will continue to teach mathematics and will simply assume legally the many duties that had already been assigned to her involving leadership… thus relieving us of onerous burdens of daily decisions."

"Good. Then it's unanimous?"

Holmes, "Aye." Wilbur, "Aye." Deere, "Aye."

"Good. We will enter into the record that Miss Eugenie Fuller was unanimously selected by The Riverside Board of Education to be Principal of Riverside High School for the following year at the salary which was posted for the position. Her designation is effective, as of this date. That concludes our business for tonight."

File photo

The Lower Canal flume across Tequesquite Arroyo in Riverside. The ornate building at the left originally housed River-side High School on the current site of Grant Elementary School at Fourteenth Street and Brockton Avenue.

**The High School classes were held
on the third floor of the building to the left**

Riverside built this imposing structure at Four-   pay for high schools. The district planned the
teenth Street and Brockton Avenue after an 1887   upper floor of this building for that purpose, and
bond issue. The state didn't then provide or help   taxed the people extra to operate it.

**A clear view of the
school building at Fourteenth and Brockton**

Principal Eugenie Fuller

Her head tipped just a bit imperiously as she dismissed the assembly and students moved excitedly to their classes. Such enthusiasm was understandable, and she shared it. Miss Fuller looked around the hall and took pride in its smell of oiled wood and the newness of folding seats, ornate wall hangings, and excellent acoustics in spite of the high and unfinished ceilings. The sunshine glistened through the windows and added a blessing to the day. One of her long-held goals had come true. She was a real Principal – not the pro tempore, not the teacher-in-charge, not the vice principal – in her own and new high school at Fourteenth and Brockton (formerly Walnut).

As she left the assembly hall and walked the short distance to her classroom, Mr. Holmes' words replayed in her head. Shortly after classes were completed for the 1886-87 school year, Mr. Holmes had evaluated her work at the Arlington School and encouraged her by saying, "You have a makeshift setting now, but you're well prepared and competent, and someday we'll get state legislation passed which will allow us to have our own high school district. When we do, you're certain to have a leadership role in Riverside High School. Welcome, Miss Fuller, to a flourishing career in Riverside."

The years had passed quickly, and she acknowledged with a nod that even before the law was enacted in the legislature in 1893, Mr. Holmes and others had moved quickly to establish the local high school program. Seven students had graduated in 1890 and several more each year since. "Such an exciting time!"

Her silk petticoats rustled beneath her skirt as she walked briskly into the classroom and beamed at her Plane Geometry students. Conversation stopped. Miss Fuller was in charge.

Mathematics was a pulsating subject for her students. Somewhat dramatic, always clear, and always expecting clear responses, she helped students sharpen their wits and become precise in their thinking. Clifford, for instance, rose to answer a question after being called upon, pondered for a moment and then said, "Well, the thought is carried..."

"And how, Clifford, is the thought carried? In a baby carriage? Take your time, think carefully, and then speak to the point."

"There was an edge to her voice, common when she wanted students to do well, knowing that they could, if only they would, stretch just a bit more toward perfection," Clifford added later in defense of her chiding.

Each student was called upon to solve a problem for the benefit of others, to recite a mathematical formula, and to show knowledge of pioneer mathematicians in the field. In every instance, participants stood by their desks or went to the front of the room to give their recitations. Several were invited to solve assigned problems on the blackboard while others studied the board work, looking for a mistake they could use to let Miss Fuller know they were focused and serious about their work.

Miss Fuller often clapped her hands when students reached 'Aha' moments, and those were the times she smilingly permitted a little raucous behavior, perhaps encouraged, while excited students congratulated each other for reaching another class milestone.

The 1896 Conference in Los Angeles
Thursday, Friday, Saturday
March 26, 27, 28

It was an honor, and the local paper touted the news that Miss Fuller, esteemed teacher and Principal of the Riverside High School, had been appointed to work with three other high school principals to give a presentation at the Southern California Teachers' Association Conference in March. It was to be held at the State Normal School, a training school for teachers, in Los Angeles during the two-week Easter vacation in 1896. This would be the fifth annual meeting of the group that had been formed from the parent organization of The California Teachers Association, instituted twenty-nine years ago.

Most of the conferences prior to this organization's formation had been held in areas near the San Francisco Bay. Educators in those vicinities were prone to think of themselves as living in the intellectual as well as the geographical center of the real California. This may have been partly because of the presence of two major universities in the area – Berkeley and Stanford, the Yale and Harvard of the West. Still, teachers in Southern California were often stung by Bay Area comments of superiority and their derogatory statements about relaxed lifestyles of teachers from the southern part of the state. These attitudes and perceptions were especially annoying to educators after spending hard-earned money and traveling hundreds of miles to attend the virtually required professional meetings.

In January 1895, President and Professor Charles H. Keyes, of the Throop Polytechnic Institute of Pasadena (and former Superintendent of Riverside schools), asked twelve high school principals in the Southern California Association to form committees and prepare material for discussion and publication at the March 1896 meeting. W. H. Housh of Los Angeles, N. A. Richardson of San Bernardino, Eugenie Fuller of Riverside, and Lewis B. Avery of Redlands were asked to work together as a committee. The focus would be on high school concerns, but they were connected to and of great interest to the other academic levels. Everyone was affected.

The men, in a gallant gesture, proposed that they meet in Riverside to spare Miss Fuller the inconvenience of traveling. She accepted with alacrity, and the group met in an alcove at the Arlington Hotel over a period of several months. Except on one occasion. Mr. Richardson had a severe leg injury, and Miss Fuller hired an associate of the Glenwood Hotel, Ed Miller, to transport her by coach to meet her colleagues in San Bernardino. The group was congenial, and the disparities in their philosophies did not deter their work. After several discussions, compromises were made, and they made an enthusiastic team.

Preparations were made for the journey to Los Angeles to attend the conference. Mr. Richardson wanted to travel by coach so that he could visit friends and relatives in communities along the way. Mr. Avery scheduled an interview for a position in a town near Los Angeles and needed to take the train a bit early. Only the members of the committee knew about Mr. Avery's plans. They had become confidantes. Mr. Housh lived only blocks away from the school. He laughed as he said that made up for the long trips to Riverside. Miss Fuller traveled by train on the 23rd and found the lodging she had arranged quite comfortable. She had a scheduled appointment to meet with Dr. Martin Kellogg, President at State University in Berkeley, to discuss an article that she had written at his request, and she also wanted to talk with him about three students who wished to matriculate in the next term. She hoped that her Galesburg mentor and long-time friend, Dr. David Starr Jordan, now President of Stanford University, might be available for conversation. She glowed from his public complimentary comments about Stanford students who had graduated from Riverside High School. High words of praise from Dr. Jordan were to be cherished. The University

Presidents looked forward to the visibility with the high school teachers and wanted to encourage them to recommend the higher education to their students. Even if their appearances were for a short time, the contacts were important.

President Keyes was to preside over the meetings, and he met with each committee prior to the call to order. Other important guests or speakers included Professor E. T. Pierce, Principal of Los Angeles State Normal School, and State Superintendent Samuel T. Black. President Keyes was ending his term with this meeting and would introduce Incoming President James A. Foshay, City Superintendent of the Los Angeles Schools, at the close of the conference on the 28th.

Concerns About Accreditation of High School Students Gaining Admission to Schools of Higher Learning was the first topic on Thursday. The atmosphere in the auditorium of 1200 teachers was tense before the committee members voiced any comments. Professor Griggs of Stanford led the discussions scheduled for Thursday, and he sensed right way that more than the usual diplomacy would be required. The committee faced questions of a controversial nature as soon as they concluded their basic presentation. Mr. Kirk of San Bernardino said that he prayed for an Abraham Lincoln to declare the emancipation of the California High Schools from the domination of the State University. He apologized to the group the next day for the vehemence of his words.

The agitation centered on university officials denying admittance of students based not only on the exam, but on whether the teacher was accredited, no matter how superior in academics. This was a particular problem when the high school program consisted of one or two teachers. The rules varied for accreditation from district to district, mainly on the decisions of the various Boards, most of whom had no college education themselves.

Mr. P. W. Kauffman, Principal of Ventura High School and a member of one of the committees, attacked the system, too. "Often," he said, "university examiners say to a student, 'Get out! Get off the face of the earth! There is no place for you!' And that is usually due to a teacher's work not being accredited, no matter how good the teacher is. Are the schools maintained for the benefit of the teachers of the State, or for the children? Answer me that!"

Additional questions and comments led to the complaint that the examiners are often severely limited in their knowledge and usually get their jobs through favoritism.

Both President Keyes and Professor Griggs called for a recess to clear the air before Eugenie and her colleagues took the floor. Dr. Jenkins of Stanford and Dr. Bailey of the State University softened the rankles and moved the day on to a happier mood with short, interesting, interspersed anecdotes, not only on Thursday morning, but throughout the three days.

The next subject on the program read: <u>What Latitude Shall be Allowed High School Pupils in Election of Studies?</u> presented by W. H. Housh, E. Fuller, N. A. Richardson, and L. B. Avery. While strong opinions were voiced, the controversy was mild, and no one raised a ruckus. One question posed whether elections by students was an acceptable ideal. If so, how could a school decide what to offer in case multiple choices were requested by students? Would offering electives shortchange the classical or general academic program? Could qualified teachers be found for electives? Who would make the final decisions about the offerings? Was any of this a good idea?

Members of the committee pointed out that most of the students who finish high school do not go on to the university, yet the curriculum is based on the expectation that students will pursue higher education. Are there some subjects that would be more valuable to young men and women in everyday life than Greek, advanced rhetoric, or trigonometry?

"Proper caution being observed," read Mr. Housh, "we would recommend the introduction of elective work into the High School course, caution referring to having enough students of a particular interest to conduct a class and have a qualified teacher. There needs to be a proficient teacher, and there must be material equipment for some classes, such as a science laboratory."

As Chairman, he continued, "We strongly recommend a wise arrangement of elective courses and elective branches, giving to those about to finish their High School education a well-guarded opportunity for preparation in special lines."

Professor Griggs accepted questions from teachers in the audience, and Mr. Housh, Miss Fuller, Mr. Richardson and Mr. Avery took turns in giving responses. In a question as to whether electives could be taken each year along with the required courses, Miss Fuller responded, "The last year should be primarily elective if all the requirements have been completed successfully."

Now it was their turn to be part of the audience and to assert their opinions. The next subject to be addressed on Friday: <u>What Shall be the Mode of Admission to the High School?</u>

The teachers became weary. Not only were there long five-hour sessions each day interspersed with short talks by featured speakers, there were keynote lectures each evening at dinner. Everyone was expected to attend. Name cards were used and socializing into late evening hours was encouraged. By Saturday evening, even the most motivated teachers wanted to go home or to pursue other activities for the last few days of their Easter vacation before making plans for Good Friday and Easter Services on April 5. With unusually large attendance, outstanding speakers, and universal membership participation, the Southern California Teachers' Association Conference was acclaimed a great success.

Riverside townspeople beamed with pride in the reflected glory of reading about Miss Fuller's attendance at the education conference in Los Angeles. Life was good. Living in Riverside was paradise, indeed.

State Normal School for Teachers in Los Angeles

Enter Arthur N. Wheelock
1898

Arthur Wheelock needed a real job. He had scouted around for something that would be fitting since growing citrus and working with water projects hadn't given him a sense of accomplishment. A townsman suggested that since Mr. Wheelock had talked often of his education and various careers, teaching at the Riverside High School just might be the answer to his dilemma. The enrollment was growing and more teachers were needed. There was fair warning, though. The Principal, Miss Fuller, was a taskmaster on high standards, and some people could find her quite demanding in her requirements. Arthur responded that he had oft heard that concern repeated around town, and he had noticed that the gossip had not affected her standing in the community.

Mr. Wheelock now thought of securing a teaching position as a personal challenge. How could the woman not see his background as anything but remarkable? After all, he had graduated from the University of Vermont in 1878, had practiced law, had taught at M.I.T., had been associated with the lumber business in Maine, had sung with the Metropolitan Opera in New York, invested in a mining venture in Utah, and invested in a citrus grove when he moved to Riverside. He had become a school trustee in a neighboring area back in 1893. Certainly, he had been part of Riverside long enough that residents admired his character and knew that he would certainly be an asset as a high school faculty member. Yes, he would apply.

The interview was set for 10:00 on a Tuesday morning. Mr. Wheelock was on time. He knew that Miss Fuller regarded lack of punctuality as completely unacceptable. He made an imposing, formal, well-dressed figure as he entered the principal's outer office with his highly polished shoes and black leather briefcase. Hat in hand and with a slight bow, he approached Miss Judson, the secretary. She noted that he was a bit out of breath, and he realized it, too. "I say, those stairs to the third floor are many and steep. Do the students get credit for calisthenics as they enter class?" Miss Judson put him at ease and ushered him across the hall to Miss Fuller's office.

"Welcome! Do come right in, Mr. Wheelock. It is pleasant to see you again. Most of our contacts have been at concerts and community meetings, so while we recognize each other, we really have an opportunity now to get acquainted." She motioned him to a chair and returned to her place behind the long, dark oak desk. At that moment, Miss Judson entered with tea, placed the tray on the desk, and said, "Excuse me for interrupting." She departed quickly. Finding himself surprisingly nervous, having the hot tea was a godsend to Mr. Wheelock, and he appreciated the social courtesy. His friend had been right. He could tell by the office decor, and by Miss Fuller's friendly yet formal manner, that the interview was to be all business – except for the tea.

They got along well, and about forty-five minutes later, Miss Fuller ended the conference by assuring Mr. Wheelock that she would recommend him to the Board of Education as a candidate to teach both Greek and Roman History for the coming term. Both of them knew well that if she recommended him, the position would be his.

As he descended the stairs to the elementary section of the school, left the grounds and walked to the trolley, he reviewed the conference and decided that Miss Fuller was bright, friendly, and lived up to her reputation. She clearly was a woman of good character and better than most he had met in the business world.

Miss Fuller gathered some papers and the geometry text from her desk and headed for class. "Yes," she said to herself, "with his academic background and professional manner and speech, he will be an asset to the faculty. I'm distressed, though, that he has been a rolling stone and has had little actual success in his ventures. He put a good face on it, but my recommendation will have some reservations. We'll see how he does over time. The Board members know him because of his work as a school trustee in Arlington. They will have the final say."

The final say placed him in a barely finished classroom located in the northwest corner of the third floor. He let students know that he would be fair and brook no nonsense. Other faculty members, especially Mrs. F. G. N. Van Slyck, took a wait-see attitude by treating him courteously, but without enthusiasm. Word got out about his many failed ventures and that caused the parents some concern. His strongest ally was Miss Fuller. Even when girls told their mothers and the mothers told Miss Fuller about his disdain for female students, Miss Fuller urged them to give him time to adjust to his new assignment.

When he approached her about the garret-like conditions of the high school site and asked her if he could make some repairs that would make the classrooms less drafty, she applauded him. When he came to her for permission to approach the Board and community members for a new building to house the students, she teamed with him to make a presentation to the Board. The members accepted the proposal for consideration.

Since the senior member of the staff, Mrs. F. G. N. Van Slyck, could barely contain her animosity towards Miss Fuller because she had been bypassed for the principalship, Miss Fuller began to rely more and more on Mr. Wheelock's level hand when she had to be off the premises during school time. Their relationship was a good one and her inner doubts dissolved.

With full support from the citizens, the Board made the decision to build a new school and bond issues passed promptly. The chosen site was vacant land at Ninth and Lime Streets in the center of town. People gloried in making suggestions in letters to The Riverside Press, and teachers all over the district were asked for their druthers for an ideal classroom and school setting. The high school staff members were happy to vacate the third floor of the school at 14th and Brockton and move into the magnificent quarters on the morning of January 6, 1902. "Yes, that's the right word – magnificent with a capital M," and she found herself mouthing the syllables as she did years ago when her father enriched her vocabulary. "Mag - ni - fi – cent! Truly magnificent!"

Mission architecture with brick walls and a tiled roof over the four entrances led to the large central assembly hall, the main focus. It was lighted from above and had seats for 400. A wide corridor ran on three sides of the assembly hall and was the entrance to twelve classrooms. Back of the assembly hall was a pleasant library room with a carefully selected library of about 1600 volumes, all supervised by a librarian who kept the doors open to students during all school hours. The three well-equipped laboratories of chemistry, physics, and botany were on the second floor over the main entrances. The basement contained lunch rooms, bicycle rooms, lavatories, and the heating apparatus. The administration offices were on opposite sides of the main entrance hall. Yes, indeed! Magnificent was the only adequate description.

After exciting tours and a special morning assembly, it was said that teachers and pupils settled down to work as if they were still in the old building. The demand for public inspection was so great that the school trustees arranged for public tours of the facilities.

Near the end of the 1902-03 term, without exposing many details, Miss Fuller asked for a year off to go on a trip to Europe. At first, Board members were reluctant, but when she told them that she had been diverting Mr. Wheelock from some of his classes so that he could assume some administrative duties and that the school would be in good hands without her presence, they agreed with alacrity because they had grown more and more to respect Mr. Wheelock's efforts. He had a formal speech pattern and every word he uttered had an air of importance. Yes, he would be the asset that Miss Fuller had predicted.

The sabbatical was forthwith granted and the town, as a whole, lauded her wish to have some personal time away from school for a little while – 'but just a little while,' they said. Only a few had tidbits of information that Eugenie planned to visit a relative in England with a Mayflower connection, a distant cousin perhaps, and that she would be accompanied by a longtime friend from Galesburg who would escort her on some site-seeing visits to the Bronte home, Anne Boleyn's gravesite, and other areas of renown in England as well as sojourns elsewhere in Europe.

Mr. Wheelock breathed a sigh of relief. While he had enjoyed teaching at the 14th and Brockton site and the new school for five years, he had begun to fret and found himself looking about for other ventures. Now that Miss Fuller and the Board invited him to assume not only the administrative duties of the high school, but to supervise the elementary program as well, even though he would still be teaching three history classes a day, he was in his element again. He found himself increasingly drawn to the administrative aspects, and he dreaded Miss Fuller's return to take over the reins again. Then what would he do?

Do? Bit by bit, he expanded his duties. He worked closely with the School Board and was happy to do the members' bidding. He joined more men's organizations in the community and became active in church doings at the Episcopalian Church, the one that important people in town attended. He had a beautiful bass voice and sang in the church, to the joy and praise of parishioners, especially since he had Metropolitan Opera credits. His delight in his work, his persona, and his efforts to win friends and influence people, perhaps unconsciously following precursors to later advice of Dale Carnegie, was paying off. Sponsorship for Arthur Wheelock was evident.

14th Street School. Known later as Grant at 14th and Brockton.

Riverside High School. Known later as Girls High School.

Miss Fuller's Return
1904

"Looky out there, Miz Fuller! Just looky out there! And it's all for you! We were told yesterday that a big crowd would be here today to show how glad they are that you're back!" The porter at the Highgrove train station had hardly been able to contain his secret, and now that it was out, he could show his glee.

Miss Fuller was speechless. She had arranged for one of the Mission Inn drivers to pick her up. It was one of the last comments she had made to Frank Miller and his traveling companions when they had arranged to meet in London just before the Inn owners completed a major shopping trip and were ready to embark for home. "Oh, mercy, my! I must gather my things. Where is my satchel?"

Right here, Ma'am. Everything's right here. I have the honor to help you. Talk about Queens of England! Looks like you're the Queen of Riverside! Now watch your step."

When she stepped down to the platform, well-wishers surrounded her – former students who could get away from work, students and their parents, teachers, and townspeople she had known for years. The senior class president was the first to speak above the whoops and hurrahs. "Welcome home! We are so glad to see you!" And with that said, senior girls brought four bouquets of long stemmed roses to lay in her arms. Quickly Miss Fuller passed her satchel, papers, and books to someone near by so that her arms could contain them all – the beautiful reds, yellows, pinks, and whites, a different color representing each high school class. She looked out to greet everyone, smiled, and then a most unusual event occurred. Tears streamed down Miss Fuller's face. No one present had ever seen her cry. "It's wonderful to be with you again. I cherish you all," she said.

Indeed, the Mission Inn coach was nearby to drive her with a Welcome Home banner flapping in the breeze – not to her home – but to the Mission Inn, the expanded Glenwood Hotel with a new name, where The Woman's Club had set up a luncheon in her honor. Tears flowed again. She couldn't help it. It was good to be back in Paradise on Earth.

Mr. Wheelock made a courtesy call. They caught up on happenings throughout the year, and she promised to be in the office soon to arrange the student schedules for the coming term. "No hurry," he said, and he meant it. He wondered how she would react to the changes he had made in her absence. "Not well," he muttered to himself on the way to his home.

And that was true. Miss Johnson, the secretary Miss Fuller chose to carry on in her absence, was on hand to greet Miss Fuller when she arrived at her office early on Monday morning. She was so relieved to see that nothing in her office had been changed since she left. "Where did Mr. Wheelock work?"

"He took over the conference room across the hall for his office. He said he didn't want to disrespect yours with his smoking and lack of organization. At first, Eugenie thought that was very decent. Then questions came. Why did he establish his own office? Why did he choose the large conference room across the corridor from hers? How did he furnish it in light of the current budget? Why were the plans she had spent hours making still in a neat stack on her desk?

"What aren't you telling me, Ruth?"

"There's little to say. He has been devoted to being here on time every day, he has taught his regular classes, he has met with students and parents about various problems, and he has been very busy making contacts in the community on behalf of the school."

"And?"

"He has taken over. He hired a temporary clerk with the approval of the Board instead of asking me to carry on all of his usual duties as well as some new ones he's assumed. He said he didn't want to interrupt our relationship, but I think he wanted to start anew with his own ideas. He has endeared himself to the board members and, being men, they react differently with him than to you. They seem to go along with any lame idea he has. Oh, excuse me, Miss Fuller."

"That's quite all right and tells me volumes. I had misgivings about going away, and it seems they were more correct than my scoffing at them."

She sat down at her desk. Ruth took the chair in front of it. "Well. I am the Principal. I'll just thank him for his services and tell him that I will resume my duties. You'll see. It will be all right."

On the surface, yes, it was all right. Mr. Wheelock said it was such a relief to have her back and that now it would free him up for other services that the Board had asked him to do in regard to supervising the elementary program. He expressed regret that he would no longer have as much time for teaching history and that they needed to interview candidates and select someone to take his place.

"Thank you, Arthur. I can do that very well on my own. I understand that you have other obligations, so dismiss the concern from your mind." Miss Fuller interviewed three individuals and made a recommendation to the Board. When the Board President accepted Miss Fuller's letter, he added, "And I'll pass this on for Mr. Wheelock's perusal. He is quite adept at helping with this kind of decision."

Miss Fuller stood beside him in stunned amazement. Her power had been usurped. He turned away and then made a polite, innocuous comment about his pleasure in knowing she was back and running the high school program with such skill.

"So it's come to that," she thought. All the plans that had been discussed over and over about her forthcoming promotion to the Office of Superintendent as soon as the city council finished wrangling and passed the long-planned city charter that would provide for a city superintendent of schools no longer included her.

That conversation had quite taken her breath away. As she walked back to school, she was oblivious to everything she passed. It was as if she were walking on an isolated pathway in the dead of night. "My reservations back in '98 were right on target. I should have remembered my father's words," she mused. 'Reputation is what others think of you; character is what you really are.' Her colleague had the reputation of being a gentleman and a scholar. She saw it differently now. "En garde," she said to herself. "En garde, Genie."

Minstrel Entertainment

John Hill's recollection of a 1904 conversation with Miss Fuller
(paraphrased from a 1954 high school reunion submission)

John got up from his desk with alacrity after he read the note that Miss Johnson, the secretary, had just delivered to him during history class. He whispered briefly to Charlie, his seat mate, "Office. Bet it's about our article in Sibyl."

There was no time to ponder why else he had been summoned, but since the advertisement announcing another minstrel show this year to raise money for the baseball team, he'd been halfway expecting trouble. Last year the show had been hilarious, raucous, and raised a fine amount of money. The students and townspeople loved it. The faculty was not amused – except for Mr. Wheelock.

John knocked on the Principal's door and was called to "Come in, please." Miss Fuller was seated behind her desk and Mr. Wheelock and Mrs. Van Slyck sat in front on either side. Miss Fuller greeted him and the others nodded and smiled. She gestured to the empty chair in the middle, and John took his seat, thinking all the while of the unfair odds in this meeting.

Miss Fuller cleared her throat. "John, as you know, I was abroad last year when you and your friends planned and executed a minstrel show, and so I completely missed your performance. I see in this month's Sibyl that you have plans for another. I shall read your advertisement.

**"Minstrel Entertainment – For the benefit of
the Athletic Association Fund – New Jokes, New Songs,
New Specialties – Watch for date Next Month"**

"John, I want to help you to raise money for the athletic fund, and I think it would be nice to have a fine concert.

"I know of your musical background and you have had earned honors heaped upon you for the professional renditions you have presented to the Tuesday Musical Club and the Woman's Club. Your gentlemanly manner immediately endears you to everyone and assures the success of your fundraising activities."

It was true, he thought, that she knew all about his reputation in the highbrow musical circles and how he could assume nice company manners and act like a so-called little gentleman.

"Here, John, is an announcement which you may choose to place in next month's Sibyl.

High School Entertainment
Mme. Johnstone Bishop
In Song Recital
Assisted by
Mr. Harry Barnhart, Miss Norma Rocca,
Miss Matie Dyer, Violin
Miss May Heller, Piano
Proceeds for the benefit of the Base Ball Fund.
High School Building
Wednesday, March 30

John was effectively trapped. Miss Fuller knew of his pleasant friendships with Matie and May, and he realized that no matter what he said, Miss Fuller's program would prevail. And he didn't want Mrs. Van Slyck to threaten to fail him again for 'inappropriate behavior and not doing his best' as she did after the last minstrel show. Mrs. Van Slyck was behind this whole conference.

Although Professor Wheelock sat silent, John noted a twinkle in his eye even though his facial expression was impassive. Mr. Wheelock had approved and passed on the minstrel show last year while Miss Fuller was on leave. "Honest," John thought to himself, "the show was clean even if it was hilarious and noisy. Walter Squires, Charlie McBean, and I were the "End Men" and Stanley "Babe" Richardson was interlocutor. The songs included a medley of the latest hits including "Rosie, You are my Posie" and the olio had the mandolin club and a sprightly march drill of a chorus of the girls in uniform. It was great."

"John, I can tell that you are thinking seriously of the possibilities. Please tell Mrs. Van Slyck, Mr. Wheelock, and me your thoughts."

"Miss Fuller, I think your suggestion is splendid," John said without batting an eye. Quickly, he had made a shrewd calculation. The Music Societies could sell the tickets – we'd have a sellout house, and he wouldn't have to do any work.

Miss Fuller breathed a visible sigh of relief. "John, we commend you for your contemplation and excellent judgment. Here is the announcement. You have permission to enter it into the school newspaper."

And that's how John Hill ceased being an impresario and actor, and that's how culture returned to the sacred precincts of Riverside High School.

The Senior Class

Riverside High School

Request the pleasure of your presence at the

Graduating Exercises,

Monday evening, June the nineteenth

Opera House,

Riverside, California

Program

Class Colors—Green and White

Music - - - - - - - - - - Orchestra
Prayer - - - - - - - - Rev. Ewd. F. Goff
Music - - - - - - - - - Orchestra
A Glimpse of Japan - - - - - - Arthur Kaneko
Holyday and Holiday - - - - Mattie Steele Singletary
The Growth of Arbitration - - - Charles F. Campbell
Selection—"On the Levee" - - - High School Glee Club
The White Man's Burden - - - - - Nellie A. Gleason
Up Mount Shasta - - - - - Arthur F. Moulton
Selection—"Until the Dawn" - - - High School Glee Club
Ella Wheeler Wilcox - - - - - Mary L. Barclay
What the Lewis and Clark Exposition Commemorates - -
- - - - - - - - - - - Edgar A. Moon
Aria-*"Una voce poco fa"*- (Selection from "The Barber of Seville")
- - - - - - - - - - - -Norma Rockhold

Presentation of Class - Eugenie Fuller, Principal of High School
Awarding Diplomas - - - A. N. Wheelock, Supt. City Schools
Benediction - - - - - Rev. Geo. H. Deere, D.D.

Motto: "Nunc Tempus Agi"

CLASS ROLL
1905

———

PAULINE MARGARET BALDWIN
EDNA BAMBERGER
CATHERINE BARTEE
FRANCES ELSIE BARBER
MARY LOUISE BARCLAY
BURTON ELWYN BLACKMAN
CECIL LA VERNE BREWER
CHARLES FRANCIS CAMPBELL
GEORGE WASHINGTON CAMPBELL
CLYDE CLIFTON CHAPMAN
MAE LOUISE DINSMORE
CHRYSSA FRASER
NELLIE ANTOINETTE GLEASON
FRANCISCO F. GONZALEZ
EULA IDELL HODSON
MATTIE MARTHA HOSP

CARL WALKER JAHN
ARTHUR KANEKO
ELLWYN H.S. KNAPP
EDNA MAY LEIGHTON
BRADLEY REVERE METCALF
ALICE MAY MITCHELL
ARTHUR FERRIS MOULTON
EDGAR ALLAN MOON
BIRDA PADDOCK
ALICE HAZEL PAPINEAU
DEXTER ALFRED RAU
ARTHUR JULIUS REHWOLD
HARVEY WILLIAM SHUMAN
MATTIE STEELE SINGLETARY
ERNEST NELSON TWOGOOD
LOVA ELDA WESTBROOK

HIGH
SCHOOL

———

THE COMMENCEMENT

———

Miss Eugenie Fuller,
Principal, Presents
the class

———

City Superintendent A. N.
Wheelock Awards
the Diplomas

———

Sixteen sweet girl graduates and an equal number of boys took part in the annual commencement exercises of the Riverside high school, held at the Loring theatre last night. Friends of the graduates came to do them honor, crowding the house to its utmost capacity, and applauding the work of the class with enthusiastic appreciation.

On the stage, in a double line in the foreground were the members of the class of 1905, their faces wearing a new and becoming dignity. The girls were as pretty and bright a flock as ever fluttered out from the protecting wing of the good old Riverside high school. In their dainty white gowns they made a charming picture. The boys were a manly lot and fairly divided the honors with the girls. At the right of the class, smiling with pardonable pride in her pupils, sat Miss Eugenie Fuller, principal of the high school, and at the opposite side of the platform was seated the city superintendent of schools, Prof. A. N. Wheelock. Arranged back of the class, rising tier above tier to the extreme rear of the stage, were the undergraduates, their minds occupied with thoughts of the night when they too will sit on the front row and receive the smiles and flowers and words of commendation.

Of course the audience broke into hearty applause when the curtain rose and disclosed the pretty scene.

The floral decorations were green and white, to carry out the class colors. Across the stage was a low hedge of white marguerites and ferns. The sides were flanked with potted ferns and palms, the boxes had a tracery of ivy and white roses, and suspended at the sides were curtains of ivy.

The program was well balanced and excellent, and was well received by the audience throughout. It was introduced by music by the orchestra and invocation by Rev. Alex Eakin.

Miss Fuller introduced as the first speaker Arthur Kaneko, the first Japanese pupil to graduate from the high school. His oration was delivered in a clear, well-modulated voice and was entitled "A Glimpse of Japan." Three years ago he visited that country, and his story was of what he saw there – the parks, the theaters, the strange methods of locomotion, the gardens, the cherry trees, the plum blossoms, the mountains, the beauties of the country and the picturesque customs of the people. In closing he touched upon the new Japan, with its new problems, but hoped that nature's gardens there might ever remain the same.

(The section that contains the additional speeches of the honor graduates is located in the appendix of this manuscript.)

Address by Miss Fuller

"The Ideal" was the keynote of the address given by Miss Fuller, principal of the high school, in presenting the graduating class. She said: "Browning has well said: 'It is not what man does that exalts him but what man would do.' If we accept this statement, then we should not be estimated so much by the yard stick of the actual as by the measuring rod of the ideal, for our aims and ambition are the true standard. The crude, imperfect outward deed is all the world can see; it does not see the shining target of which the arrow fell so short. The greatness of a man depends upon the swiftness with which his dream outruns his reality; upon the proportion with which his plans overtop his performance; it depends upon his unfinished work and not his finished. In this view of the ideal there is no room for listless musing, for fruitless holding of the hands. These higher scenes must hover over fields of toil. As the beautiful landscape with its lines of river and lake and shore is made by long chiseling and steady pressures, by ages of glacier crush and grind, by scour of floods, by centuries of sun and storm, so a beautiful life, a

successful life is the attainment of years of toil, of devotion to principle, of sacrifice. Faithful performance of the daily tasks whatever they be, cheer under the drill and press of heavy burdens, grace to meet discouragements and defeats, ambition, the power of self control, and self denial—these are the prime qualities. The mothers' oft repeated advice and pleadings, the threadbare precepts of the school room, the platitudes from the pulpit and the proverbs of the nation all point to the same thing. The nobler the life and the higher the ideals of that life the more essential these qualities. The achievements of all great men have come through the same source, the plod and the drill and long disciplines of toil accompanied by discouragements.

"Columbus was obedient to his ideal, and through self denial and hardships, and with indomitable courage on his part a new world sprung into existence; likewise the Pilgrims, and that new world became the birthplace of civil and religious freedom. It was a lofty ideal that actuated John Brown, and four millions of slaves at last lifted their faces to the sun. Abraham Lincoln was obedient to a lofty ideal and the flag of the Union, no stars blotted out, no stripes torn asunder waves from Polar sea to Southern cross.

"So with the humbler life—its high aim and its standard consecrate it. The smallest pool has its water from heaven and its gleam from the sun and it holds the stars in its bosom, as well as the ocean.

"I beseech you, keep your ideals; keep them high and bright. In mature life they may seem to become dim; contact with the worst and most selfish side of life, depreciated standards in business and society may tarnish them, but keep on for the encouragement is that some day you may accomplish the object of your endeavors. Remember that ideals are of God. Keep them high and bright in spite of failure frequent and humiliating—in spite of defeat and disaster. They are not false lights that beckon you nowhere; they are not malign spirits that lure you to destruction. They are flashes from heaven, gleams of the eternal light that will lead you at last to him in whom there is no darkness at all."

And then, when the class had passed about and received the precious sheepskins which represented four years of earnest effort in their high school, the orchestra struck into a swinging march and the boys of the Junior class brought on the first bouquets of the shower of beautiful flowers. Numberless trips were made back and forth by the bearers of these sweet messages, and bouquets and baskets and clusters of beautiful carnations, roses, magnolias, sweet peas, and other flowers, were placed in the arms and about the feet of the graduates. It was a beautiful scene, as the floral wealth of California's early summer was showered upon the happy recipients, and the proudest moment most of those lives had ever known.

And when all was over, and a tender blessing had been asked by the aged Dr. Deere, the stage became a scene of chaos and confusion, as many friends crowded forward to shake hands and offer congratulations over the banks and piles of flowers. (One added bit of interest: the ceremony started late as usual – approximately eight p.m. – and lasted until after 11.)

Perhaps not 1905, but a typical graduation scene, often at the Loring Theatre (Opera House)

Women's Right to Vote
October, 1911

In January 1878, Senator A. A. Sargent of California had introduced a national suffrage amendment in Congress. Congressmen were unwilling to risk their seats by trying their luck with an electorate that included women. The amendment was buried in committee for nine years and when the full Senate finally considered it in 1887, it was defeated by a vote of 16-34. Suffragists turned to their states and hoped to gain the vote in their home territory and to keep at it until there was universal suffrage in the United States.

The first statewide vote in California came in 1896. Failure resulted. The women kept working. Women's Clubs proliferated, teas were held, speakers lectured, and by 1911, the Progressives in both major parties proposed State Amendment No. 8 which resulted in Proposition 4 being placed on the ballot. Fervent arguments for and against pitted women against women, church and family members against each other, and rhetoric increased to a boiling point. At last, October 10 arrived.

That Tuesday was tense. Throughout the day, the men in California would decide if their wives, mothers, sisters, daughters, and all the women in the state had the right to vote at the next election. Many wives gave their husbands an extra pat on the shoulder that morning as they left the house. Mothers looked at their grown sons with that stern gleam in their eyes. The pressure was on. Throughout the day, women gathered in little pockets as if talking would make it all come true. Many held hands and prayed. Mothers wheeled baby buggies on the street because it was just too hard to sit at home alone and wait.

There was another side to the story. Some viewed that voting for Proposition 4 was unnecessary, and absolutely harmful to the society, in general, and to the family unit, in particular. Tempers flared and vicious comments were made that just saying sorry later could never make friendships whole again. Wealthy, married matrons were the worst, and, although they may have been echoing words of husbands, the venom coming from women against women was vehement. No milquetoasts here. Many women in Riverside were castigated openly, but the poison was in spreading rumors and belittling, often behind the scenes, the explanations that favored the vote. Two women got so involved in their conversation at the market on Tuesday morning that they didn't realize their voices had loudened, and that several others, with grocery lists in hand, heard every word.

"Did you hear that Miss Fuller talked to a group of girls in her office last Thursday about how they could do anything they set their minds to? Supposedly, she was encouraging them to stay in the algebra class even though their teacher had recommended that they switch to an easier class. But you and I – "

"Yes, you and I know – the whole town knows – that she is inciting them to compete with the boys, and you know they'll never use algebra in a hundred years."

"Waste of time. And speaking of boys, I heard from Elizabeth that three girls got in the family way over the summer."

"Yes, I heard all about it, too. One went to Los Angeles for you know what, and the other two are living out of town. Shame. Shame. Such good parents, too. Always went to church."

"And it all goes back to lack of discipline at the school last year. I hold Miss Fuller responsible. The Superintendent's idea of separating the girls from the boys during school is long past due. Of course, she's against it..."

"Miss Fuller, you mean."

"Of course. She told my husband that girls should have the same opportunities as the boys, and she really made a fuss when he took Elizabeth out of the Latin class anyway. He said he felt like a kid who had done something wrong by the time she got through admonishing him."

"That's Miss Fuller for you. If Proposition 4 passes, there'll be no living with her."

"I tell you, something has to be done. I've been talking to a board member candidate, and he agrees. He says they're working on it."

The conversation ended abruptly when the grocer, standing behind the counter and waving to a departing customer, said in an embarrassed voice, "Now, yes Ma'am, what can I get for you today?"

Others in earshot said nothing at the time, but the homes were abuzz that evening when the gossip was repeated. It was bound to grow. Gossip does.

———

Eugenie eyed each man who entered the school that day. Each teacher. Each janitor. Each parent. Each School Board member. The Superintendent. She found body language, facial expressions, and eye messages easy to read. She kept her opinions to herself and did not get into wondering and guessing throughout the day as results were predicted. Students and teachers alike knew that comments should be reserved until the polls published.

There was no doubt as to her position. She had asserted her concerns with her students for years that until women students had the same rights as the young men, choices for careers and businesses and professions would be less attainable. Not impossible, but the barriers deterred many a young woman, often strongly influenced by her parents, to do less than she could. The vote would encourage responsibility for taking positions on issues and that would lead to decisions not possible without it.

Still, she didn't mention it in her classes or in student contacts that day. It was too late, she thought, to change men's opinions. Now it was time to wait and see as a steady stream of men passed through each precinct voting place and left his decision on paper whether women in California deserved the right to vote and whether they could be trusted with it.

The meeting at the Woman's Club (Main and Eleventh Streets) after school told a different story. It was a time for assuring and reassuring, a time for stories about how they'd extracted promises from the men in their families, a time for crossing fingers and having tea and sharing nervous laughs. The nightmare was about to be over.

———

By the next day, everyone was talking about it. Proposition 4 had passed. True, the vote was close, by only 3587 votes, but it passed everywhere except in the San Francisco area. All that work in going door to door, all those social calls and afternoon teas, all those meetings at the Woman's Club and the WCTU — the Woman's Christian Temperance Union building, all those urgent conversations with any man who would stand still long enough to listen — even for a few sentences until he cut you off with his promise to cast his vote for woman suffrage in California, all those efforts had been rewarded. The men were heroes. Since it wasn't possible to know for sure who voted in favor, all men were treated as if they had. That wasn't possible, of course, since the vote was so close. In spite of the opposition from The Los Angeles Times and the bitter vitriol that appeared in other newspaper columns, the women in California had gained political status.

———

That evening, Eugenie penned a long letter to Emily, citing chapter and verse of the town's doings and the reactions to the election. She noted that she had received praise and congratulations from many — mostly students and young families and former Galesburgers — and bristles from others, but not to her face. Still, she knew. Also, Eugenie knew that all of Galesburg would get the news and that Abraham would be furious.

Conflict
1911

"Arthur, I am unalterably opposed to your actions."

"Of course you are, Eugenie. You have always been emphatic in your views and believe you know what's best for society. You have become much more adamant through the twelve years we have worked together. I'm telling you. This community has changed. People are not nearly as pedantic, not as moralistic, not as honest, not as patriotic as they were even ten, fifteen years ago. Their children are not as well supervised and get into mischief that we educators can do nothing about, but while they are charges in our school, we can temper the problems."

"By separating the girls from the boys so that they have an artificial view of the world that needs both men and women to work together? By curbing their eruptive passions artificially through separation rather than guiding them to discipline themselves because they know it's the right thing to do?"

"You've read my speech that I've delivered to several organizations and to the Present Day Club only a few days ago. The Board has published and circulated it, and..."

"How can you sit there and tell me your comments are for the good of the high school students? Here is what you said, and I quote:

'...We shall adopt segregation of boys and girls in secondary schools as an important means of conserving the real purpose of education – socially efficient, manly men and womanly women...'

"And here,"

'...the environment and education of the boy should wholly make for manliness, just as that of the girl should make for womanliness... Something of virility is lost to the boy whose high school life is passed in a school in which girls and women teachers predominate. It is even a more serious matter for the girls. Something of the bloom, the charm of girlhood and young womanhood is endangered in the rather boisterous atmosphere of a mixed school...'

Eugenie looked directly at him and said, "This is not an educator speaking. The girls should have equal opportunities for academic choices. They already have so many inescapable barriers because they can't participate or practice in most fields."

"You did."

"Galesburg supported and encouraged girls and boys equally. Even without the legal vote, we were respected and treated the same. So were we in Riverside until a few years ago."

"Are you referring to 1898 when I joined the school system?"

"Well, I wasn't, but perhaps that is when it happened."

"One more thing, Eugenie, before I must leave you. Tone down your rhetoric about woman suffrage and equal rights and emancipation for the high school girls. It's not womanly, and people are talking."

"You know, Arthur, a very dear friend in Galesburg made just about the same remarks to me many years ago. I resented it then, and I resent it now."

"Very well, I must go to another meeting. We can continue our conversation later." He rose, bowed slightly in a baronial manner, picked up his hat and walking stick, and quietly pulled her office door behind him as he left.

Segregation of Sexes In The Public High Schools
by Arthur N. Wheelock

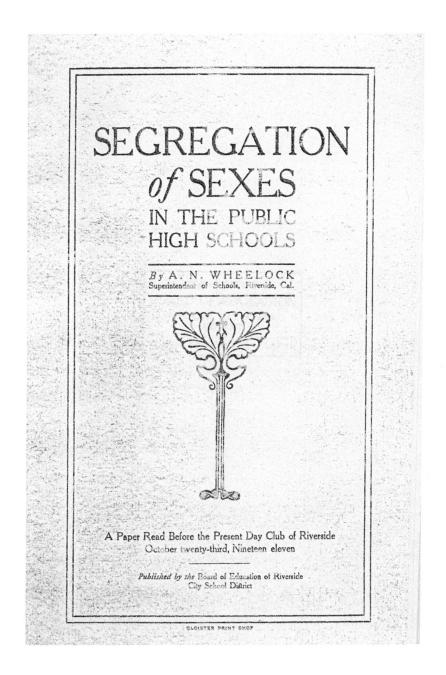

SEGREGATION *of* SEXES IN THE PUBLIC HIGH SCHOOLS

By A. N. WHEELOCK
Superintendent of Schools, Riverside, Cal.

A Paper Read Before the Present Day Club of Riverside
October twenty-third, Nineteen eleven

Published by *the* Board of Education of Riverside
City School District

CLOISTER PRINT SHOP

ARTHUR NEWHALL WHEELOCK
Superintendent of Schools, Riverside, Cal.

140

Miss Fuller's Headache

Miss Fuller's thoughts hung in the air. Her head was ripping apart with another migraine – the second one this week. She left the office and told Ruth that she was going to the arbor for a little peace and quiet. Ruth quickly made a wet compress for her, and Eugenie really appreciated the cold wetness as she slid into a tilt-back lawn chair and placed the pad over her eyes and forehead.

"This vine-covered arbor offers tranquility and solace and privacy," she thought to herself. "The slightest breeze stirs the bougainvillea and shadows dance in the afternoon and bring coolness and peace. What an excellent idea the students had when they petitioned for a shady alcove in the quad – a place where they could hold the school's club meetings on unbearably hot days. It had become a respite for staff, too, and teachers often met here with parents when the classrooms were too hot to sit comfortably and carry on conversations."

Miss Fuller's coiffed head was throbbing, throbbing. She turned the compress over and used the rest of its coolness. Gradually, the pain subsided just a bit. "Please, body, please get over this," she pleaded earnestly with herself. "I am to meet with Mr. Wheelock at 4:00. It's not going to be pleasant."

Time passed – she didn't know how long. Maybe half-an-hour. She must have drifted off and was a little confused when she heard voices. "Meredith, come here. I have to talk to you."

"Here?" a girl's voice answered. "Why don't we just start walking home, and you can tell me on the way. Mother doesn't like it when I'm late getting home from school." And then Meredith looked at her friend, Patricia. She could tell that Patricia was near tears, that her face was flushed, and that she was literally shivering in hundred-degree heat.

"Land's sake, Patricia, what's the matter? You look awful. What's the matter?"

"Meredith, I am in so much trouble, I don't know what to do. I think Father and Mother will kill me. I don't dare go home. I'm ashamed to face them. I've done so much wrong that they can't forgive me, and I can't forgive myself. And I have no one to talk to or to help me. I think I might be, might be – uh, you know."

Meredith stood there, aghast, stupefied. Not her friend! Not her friend since first grade! "You missed a whole day of school and you went to the desert with Bill Jacoby, didn't you? You said you might. But Patricia! He's married."

"I know, I know. Twice. But he's so good looking, and he has this great car and he said he really liked me and wanted to show me a good time, and I didn't think it would go this far. Father will kill me. He'll kill me – and if he doesn't, I'll kill myself."

"Come let's sit over here. It's a bit more shady. We have to figure out what to do."

"I'll have to run away, Meredith – but I don't have any money. I don't have anyone to run to. I am so scared, and there's no one to help me. No one." As they moved a little further into the alcove, they saw Miss Fuller with disheveled hair and a wet rag in her hand trying to get upright in the yard chair. Both girls were transfixed. The world had just ended for both of them. "Oh, Miss Fuller! Oh, Miss Fuller! What – what can we say?"

"For starters, you can say it isn't so and mean it. Come, girls, sit down. There's always someone to help you. Please sit down on the bench next to me. I have been sitting here nursing a big headache. Now the three of us have a catastrophic one. Now, let's just sit real still for a few minutes and gather our wits."

"But Miss Fuller. You know how upset my mother gets when I'm even a few minutes late. She will be out looking for me and making a scene all the way from our house to the office. Please – I'm upset, too."

"Calm down, Meredith. We'll deal with that problem later. I'm supposed to be in a conference with Mr. Wheelock at this very moment, so I think that we are all being sought by frustrated people."

"Miss Fuller, I'm sorry to disappoint you and I know you must be very angry with me and please don't tell my mother and father and please – my words were meant for Meredith to hear, not you." Patricia's words ran together – no pauses.

"Oh, yes, I'm disappointed all right, and I'm not just angry; I'm furious with that scoundrel Jacoby. He was a problem in school years ago, and now he's a bigger problem in the community. If he thinks for one minute that I'll allow him to sully the reputation of one of my girls, you girls know better. But I'm not following my own advice here to be calm. Let us walk to my office as nonchalantly as we can. My secretary will take care of notifying everyone about our being delayed, and I want you girls to calm your wits and help to carry this off without arousing any suspicions."

"You're going to help me? After all the mean things I've done – like writing notes in study hall, and leaving school without permission and talking about you being mean and strict?"

"Don't you think those issues are a bit too petty for us to even think about right now? We have a serious problem here, and we're going to get busy and solve it. It's going to be untenable for a while, but we will prevail. Now. Let's walk across the Quad laughing and talking until we get inside my office door. Then you can be upset again, but keep your voices subdued."

As they entered the office, Miss Fuller with considerable enthusiasm said, "Ladies, I think your idea to promote the next assembly with more emphasis on local history is most interesting. I will need a few minutes more of your time. Miss Johnson, please relay our regrets for punctuality to the parents of these students and give my regrets to Mr. Wheelock. We need to reschedule the conference. Students, come right this way." And the door closed.

Miss Johnson, the secretary, – Ruth in informal dialogue – had no time to ask Miss Fuller about her painful migraine. She could tell, however, that something was amiss, and she was long experienced on handling situations diplomatically without knowing the details.

Both girls broke into sobs. Miss Fuller waited quietly. "Meredith, you are Patricia's friend, and I appreciate your loyalty to her. However, if your mother arrives and asks that you go home, I have no reason to withhold her request. For the time being, though, I am asking that you refrain from discussing your friend's dilemma. It is out of character for me to ask you to be devious. It is in character for me to ask you to trust Patricia, her parents, and me to make appropriate decisions on her behalf. I must advise you that you are not at liberty to discuss this matter with others. We do not need rumors to abound, and we do not need the destruction of anyone's reputation."

"You have my word, Miss Fuller. You and Patricia both have my word."

"Very well, Meredith. You are a true friend. Now, Patricia, I am going to ask that you and your parents come to my home this evening at half past six. I do not want you to be suffering so throughout the night, and I do not want to discuss this matter further at school. I will ask Miss Johnson to make the arrangements. You may both go now." Neither girl moved.

Miss Fuller walked to the other side of the room to close the window and then put on her hat. She put her hands on the hands of both girls. "Girls, you are not the first young women to deal with this problem. You will suffer through this and be stronger for it. Right now, you are right. It's the worst moment in your life. You will survive. I promise. You are both now excused. Good day." Miss Fuller swept out of the room and stopped to talk to Miss Johnson.

"I don't believe it," Patricia said. "That was Miss Fuller. The strictest person who never does anything wrong and gets after us for the least little thing."

Meredith nodded her head in agreement. "And all the time, she truly understands. I think she is the most wonderful person in the world."

When the girls passed the secretary's desk, Miss Johnson called out to them. "Meredith, your mother stopped by to see if you were detained at school, and I explained to her that you were talking with Miss Fuller about a school project and that you would be home within the hour. She was very pleased to know that you are in Miss Fuller's good graces.

"And Patricia, here is a note for you to take to your parents. Miss Fuller wrote it out and asked me to give it to you. And you girls have a pleasant dinner and evening. And don't forget homework," she added with a giggle.

"Aw, Miss Johnson, you've gone and ruined your goodbye. You have a pleasant evening, too, and you will – because you don't have to do homework."

"Goodbye, Meredith. Goodbye, Patricia."

As Meredith and Patricia walked out the door, Miss Johnson scooted her fancy-shoed feet back and forth on the wooden plank floor under her desk as she was prone to do when she was a bit anxious and wondered to herself what that last hour was all about. No need to worry. Miss Fuller will take care of it. She always does.

Miss Ruth P. Johnson,
Secretary to Miss Fuller and Mr. Wheelock

Courtesy Ruth Johnson

Note: Aside from Miss Fuller and Miss Johnson, the names in this chapter and succeeding two chapters have been fictionalized.

An Evening Conference

Eugenie scarcely had time to refresh herself after her brisk walk home from school and before her guests arrived. She hastened to wash her face and redo her hair, and then she added a flounce to her blue plaid skirt. Her headache? Hard to tell. Numb was more like it. But if it was going to cause her anguish, it would just have to wait until her guests departed.

At the same time that Eugenie was brewing tea and arranging cookies on a plate, the Fentons walked a bit slowly as they approached her home. It would not be seemly to be early, but it certainly wouldn't do to be late. Mr. Fenton pulled out his watch and shaded it from the glare of the waning sun. Yes, I do believe that it is time." Mr. and Mrs. Fenton walked together, with Patricia just a few steps behind. Hearing a rap-rap on the screen door, Eugenie quickly greeted the family and ushered them inside. "Well, Robert – and Emily, it is so good to see your faces again! You are both looking well and I hear that the business is prospering under your direction, Robert.

"I owe most of that to you, Miss Fuller. Your insistence that I take math courses that would bless me later has certainly been that – a blessing."

"Oh, my, listen to him, Emily and Patricia! I could do no less. When I heard that he was going to take over the hardware store after his father died, I simply insisted that he polish his skills since he had left school years before. Come. Come sit over here. You will get a wisp of breeze as we get close to sunset."

Patricia was going to linger back, but Miss Fuller had none of that. "Right over here, Patricia. You are our subject this evening, and we want to have you right here so we can support you and be close to you." Patricia hung her head at first, then looked directly at her parents.

"Mother, Father, I guess you know that Miss Fuller wants this meeting because I have sinned. I am so overwhelmed, but Miss Fuller is trying to give me courage to confide in you."

The parents looked expectantly at Miss Fuller, but her eyes were on Patricia. "Patricia, my dear young lady, you are a treasure chest of courage right now. I am so proud that we can all sit here together and solve this dilemma."

Dilemma? By now, both parents shifted their positions and Mrs. Fenton sat on the edge of the sofa and leaned forward to the point that Mr. Fenton motioned for her to sit back. "You are so close to the edge, my dear, you may take a tumble." Nervous laughter all around. Just the same, Mr. Fenton's jaw muscles were twitching. "Come now, Miss Fuller, you've had a long day. I know this unusual visit concerns more than failing a test or flirting with the boys."

"You're right, Robert, and you know me well. It's just that I want to ascertain that we all know that we love Patricia and that we don't want to do or say things that will harm her more than she has already harmed herself." Silence.

"Mother, Father, I have to confess to you that I have played hooky from school, and..."

Exclamations started, but Patricia interrupted. "Let me finish and get it all out, or I think I shall just explode." Miss Fuller murmured, "Let her finish, Robert," and Patricia continued.

First came a repeated comment that she had played hooky, then she explained that she had been invited to go to Desert Hot Springs for a dip in one of the spas, and then she told of coming back to school just in time for dismissal.

"How did you get there?"

"By car."

"Whose car?"

"Bill Jacoby's."

"When was this?"

"A couple of months ago."

"Who else was with you?"

"Delores."

"And who else?"

"Tom Hillman."

"Those are married men!"

"I know."

"Why?"

"We thought it would be fun. We didn't see the harm in it."

"But you knew it was wrong."

"Yes."

"And that we would be disappointed."

"Yes."

"Crushed."

"I thought you wouldn't know."

"And why are we just finding out about this?"

"I was telling Meredith about how bad I feel about it, and Miss Fuller overheard part of what we said."

"Robert, Emily, the girls and I talked, and I made the decision to ask you here to discuss the matter – partly because it's not appropriate to discuss this at school and partly because Patricia is suffering so much, I did not want to postpone this conversation. Let me get the tea, and I'll leave the three of you to talk about this privately."

When Eugenie returned with the tea service, it took only a glance to see how devastated both parents were. Their comments and attitudes were mixed. Some accusatory to Patricia, some negative towards Delores, anger directed at the men involved and humiliation that Miss Fuller had to know about this.

"You will need to consult a physician to determine the status of her health." That was the bombshell of the evening. More questions. More anguish. "Now, I must speak bluntly to all of you. First ascertain Patricia's state of health. If she's fine, then this conversation need go no further and it will be as if it never occurred."

"And if she's not?"

"Then you, as her parents, and dear Patricia will have some soul-searching decisions to make. I've been thinking on the matter this afternoon. There is a wonderful program at Berkeley for young women to matriculate and enjoy a season abroad for cultural studies in several countries. The class may be full, but if you decide you want me to, I will contact Benjamin Wheeler and ask for an exception. Patricia is eligible by both her age and her fine academic work – and my recommendation."

As was Miss Fuller's noted pattern in working with people, the anger dispersed, and the four suffered together as they retraced and reviewed the innocuous events that spiraled into this regrettable circumstance. The teapot emptied. By twilight, the meeting was over. Emily and Eugenie embraced. Eugenie took Patricia's hand and placed it on her father's.

"Parents, our society is harsh with young, gullible girls. Patricia – just look at her – is beautiful with her long golden tresses and soulful eyes. She's very fragile right now, so avoid casting aspersions. She's your flesh and blood. Instead, save those for the predator who sought her out and violated her. 'What's done is done and cannot be undone.'

"Remember, there is no problem that will destroy us. Stay very calm and do what you must, and continue to love each other. No act of anguish is worth jeopardizing that love and the determination to survive. If you need me further, I am at your service."

"Thank you, Miss Fuller. Thank you. I don't know what to say."

"You have all handled this situation with courage and expressed yourself well. Now just go home, get some sleep and you'll deal with this tomorrow. Patricia, I expect to see you at school and attentive to your teachers."

"Yes, Miss Fuller."

Shortly after, the screen door closed and Eugenie carried the empty teacups to the kitchen. The headache had returned in full force.

Miss Fuller Talks to William

Miss Fuller approved of herself in the long mirror in the entryway, picked up her parasol from the hallway rack and quickly went about her errands on Saturday morning. Her main goal was to go to the Citrus Fruit Exchange, and she was there by ten o'clock when she knew all the workers would be busy with customers or wholesale clients. She wandered about the crates of oranges and lemons and nodded to friends and strangers alike. Yes, now that the tourist trade was flourishing, and new people were settling in town, nearly half of all the people she saw that day were strangers. She was about to mentally comment on this matter when she spotted Bill Jacoby stacking crates of citrus that would be loaded onto the train for its afternoon run.

"William, it is imperative that I speak with you for a few minutes. Would you like for me to get a reprieve from your duties from Mr. Driscoll?"

"No Ma'am, that won't be necessary. I will just work a little longer in the day to make up for it, if need be. How may I help you, Miss Fuller?"

"William, let us stand over there under the tree where there is some shade. Even with the parasol, the sun seems driven to melt everything but the beautiful citrus. You must be working very long and hard these days, and you seem to thrive on the heat."

"Yes, Ma'am. Our orchards are prospering. I am fortunate to be able to work in the open air and mostly, I supervise myself."

"Yes. That's a bonus for you, I'm sure."

"Now that we're in the shade, would you like to sit over here on the bench?"

"Thank you, no. What I have to ask and say demands standing. I shall be quite precise. Perhaps you are aware of the purpose of my visit."

"No, not really, but I'll be glad to help you in any way, Miss Fuller. Tell me – "

Miss Fuller interrupted, "No, you tell me how you can be so morally corrupt as to be taking young ladies in my school out for rides in your automobile! And tell me, too, what made you think you could do such deeds with impunity?"

"Now see here, Miss Fuller, I'm not in your school anymore. I know you always disliked me even though I tried my best to please you." He flushed and looked down to the ground. "Well, most of the time."

"William, you are evading my questions. I have it on good authority that you have taken a student – at least one student – away from her duties at school, and your intentions were not honorable. I am here to let you know that the truth will out if you do not take an honorable role henceforth. I am here to tell you that if authorities of the law must be notified, I will do that because I will not have you and your friends enticing my students from class again."

"Miss Fuller, I just wanted to have a good time, and I didn't do anything wrong and..."

"You lie. You lie with such a righteous look on your face. Let me be clear. I will notify authorities that you are not to be in or near the school premises unless you are in the company of your wife or children. Let me be clear. If there is another instance of this dastardly behavior toward my students, I shall personally discuss the matter with your wife – and Clara doesn't deserve to be hurt further – and your employer."

"But Miss Fuller..."

"Don't Miss Fuller me. I strongly advise you to give restitution to the parents of this young girl – and I hope there is only one young girl involved, but I shall leave that matter up to you, your wife, and the parents – along with authorities of the law. Have I made myself clear, William?"

"Yes, Miss Fuller."

"Good Day, William." Miss Fuller began to walk away. A step or two later, she heard William say something barely audible. She turned. "Yes, William? You were saying?"

"Oh, I was just sayin' goodbye, Miss Fuller, and wishin' you keep doing well."

"I shall, William. Thank you. Now you take care of business."

"Dang!" He thought to himself. "She's still so pretty and so smart and when you do something wrong, she makes you feel like squat even when you're a grown man. I'm in deep trouble now, and she makes me feel like an ornery little kid. If she was still talkin' to me, she'd say something like, 'Well, William, now you must pay the piper.' I wonder if she was talking about Patricia or..." A tourist asked a question about the different posters on the crates, and that was a welcome diversion.

He worked furiously the rest of the day, but his troubled mind and queasy stomach had the upper hand.

Transitions
1911 – 1912

As water wars stabilized and Riversiders were assured of water for their thirsty orange groves and other crops, population boomed. The school enrollments grew so fast that the local paper was full of instances of how education was being affected by the crowded classes. The grand plans for the new Polytechnic High School built on sixteen acres in the Tequesquite Arroyo were near fruition and would be ready for occupancy by the boys in the fall of 1912, thanks to the community's generous financial support.

1912 was to be a banner year for the teachers, too, because the tenure law for teachers would go into effect midyear, thus sparing teachers the fear of losing their positions because of parents who complained any time their children were dissatisfied with the programs, rules, or discipline decisions and subsequently wanted the teachers dismissed.

As newcomers came to town, they were not as likely to settle into the written and unwritten rules of the community going back to early settlement times, and turmoil had become more common.

Two seats on the Riverside City School Board changed in 1911.

The classes were separated in 1911 by scheduling the boys in the mornings and girls in the afternoon "because of limited space." Miss Fuller protested furtherance of the plan that would send the boys to the new high school and keep the girls at the established one. Why not have two coeducational schools with the same programs? No. The new high school would provide a manual arts and vocational program for boys who were not believed to merit encouragement for college programs. Courses would be offered to girls that would promote womanliness –

homemaking classes, including cooking and sewing. No longer would they be required to take higher math or foreign language classes. The town was torn about the issue, but Mr. Wheelock prevailed with the support of the Board of Education (including two newly elected members with agendas for change) and a small but influential group of the local population.

The year was difficult. Boys left notes in their desks in the mornings; girls found them and wrote answers in the afternoon classes and stuffed the notes way back in the desks for the boys to find next morning. There was much giggling and inattentiveness in both sessions, and it took some time for the teachers to ferret out the reasons.

One girl, a daughter of a popular, wealthy physician, cheated on an examination and Miss Fuller, after a conference with her, told her that her punishment would be to make a public apology in front of the entire student body on a day when all boys and girls would be together for an assembly. The girl told her father and the father came to school and protested the matter with Miss Fuller, to no avail, prompting the father to take his concerns to a member of the Board who would be sympathetic to his complaints. Nevertheless, the girl did go to the front of the assembly, admitted cheating and offered an apology. It was said that some students' grades suddenly plummeted, but there was no sign of cheating for months afterward.

Over the term, high school teachers became exhausted, edgy, and unhappy because of having to share their classrooms for double duty assignments and because they were without extra remuneration to compensate for the difficulties. The Board ascertained that the situation was temporary and that funds were scarce because of the required innovations for the boys at the new high school. The only extra people hired were on-site janitors and groundskeepers because Superintendent Wheelock was firm about the pristine appearance of the premises.

Since 1907, when the city charter passed and the Superintendent was formally appointed, elementary school boundaries began to change.

At first, parents made a request for their children to go to a specific school and it was granted. Then elementary school boundaries began to change, and segregation of Anglos from other students became more noticeable as new schools were built to accommodate the burgeoning enrollments. Transfers for Anglo students became increasingly common. Students with Mexican, Chinese, Japanese, or Negro heritage did not qualify. These quiet changes were looked upon with favor by the power structure of the community, and the Superintendent's popularity increased.

All agreed that the education programs and philosophies in Riverside were in transition.

Remembering Christmas

Miss Fuller was not so bubbly near the beginning of Christmas vacation. The past few weeks had been crammed with activities, students were excited, and some were unruly so close to the holiday period. Eugenie stopped for tea and crumpets at the Blue Tea Room, and Mrs. Bennett gave her a mouth watering delicacy to enjoy later as they exchanged Christmas greetings and said goodnight. Eugenia's empty abode was somber and needed cheering, so she started a fire and sat down to rest a bit. The lilting flames and the crackling wood soothed her into a dreamlike state and, almost immediately, Eugenie relived a Christmas past.

Charlotte, Emily, and I stood at the top of the stairs where we hugged and went to our own beds. All the rituals had been followed. The stockings were hung on the mantel, close, but not too close to the chimney. Although the coal and logs would turn to embers during the night, the chimney area stayed hot and kept the upstairs warm. Making gingerbread cookies in the forenoon was fun and decorating them with sugar, nuts and raisins even more so. By late afternoon, they were crisp and hard enough to hang on the spruce tree in the parlor. The conversations of my parents and guests and occasionally of Charlotte and Emily made the evening almost dreamlike with the soothing sounds.

Just before supper, I read my own special verses from the Bible as I took my turn in the big circle in the room. Everyone in the family read their special choices each year, and we memorized everyone's recitations and helped out if someone stumbled over a word. Guests selected their own, and the Christmas story was told with tiny, high voices, gruff and serious tones, and halting words from people who fought poor vision or where the flickers of the lamp darted on the walls instead of on the pages. Then supper was served. That meant that everyone had a task as the tables were set and the pitchers and bowls were brought in from the kitchen and placed just so. Tonight was such a feast. Mouth watering aromas had fled the kitchen all day as the turkey roasted and the dishes to go with it were made. So it was going to be especially hard, once we were seated, to listen to prayers from everyone at the table while the food got cold. Papa was as good as Santa Claus tonight. He said a brief Thank You to the Lord, looked around the table and said, "We'll save the rest of the thank you prayers for after dessert tonight. The Lord, I believe, wants us to enjoy this food right away."

We all clapped. The two young boys who were visiting with their parents – well, much younger than I – began to whistle, but they were cut off sharply with a shaking of heads and piercing looks. The Christmas dessert pudding was made of bread, milk, honey, and raisins, and covered with a thick, fluffy cream that had been beaten ahead of time and placed out on the back porch until the right moment. Papa passed a vial of brandy for the men to add to the confection. The prayers were not forgotten and everyone had a turn. Then Mama went to the organ and began to play Silent Night. It was a magical Christmas Eve. Before the last evening prayer, Papa read <u>The Visit of Saint Nicholas</u> – a happy tradition he started before we could understand the words.

All too soon, the guests who lived in a reasonable distance bade their good nights, and the ones staying over were escorted to their quarters. A goodnight kiss and a light touch on the head and shoulders meant that Emily and Charlotte and I were directed to retire without a word being said.

For a long time, I lay abed thinking about the day and the excitement was too much to allow for sleep. I wondered if I would really get the gift I yearned for, hoped that Emily and Charlotte's wishes will come true, and hoped that mother and father will enjoy the comforter we girls made for them. We crocheted three dresser doilies for Reverend and Mrs. Beecher who would be with us for at least two more days while he's preaching in

Knoxville, and I hoped that they really would like them and wouldn't see the mistakes we made.

Yes, I heard noises, but stayed right in bed and listened. Perhaps Santa Claus is really here. Perhaps people running from slavery who still pass this way and stay in the basement of the barn are arriving – or leaving. Perhaps some people are lost because of the snowdrifts, and they're going to ask Papa for help. Perhaps...

Before it seemed the night had time to pass, Charlotte and Emily jumped on my bed. "Wake up, wake up, you silly ninny! It's time to go downstairs. Come on! Come on!" From the top of the stairs we looked down on a joyous sight: a crackling fire with logs piled high, our ribbon and cookie bedecked tree with wrapped packages piled around it, a heap of hot cakes on the dining room table and mugs of steaming hot chocolate just poured. It surely is a Merry Christmas! It is so hard to use our manners and be polite right now.

"Hurry down, girls!" Papa called out to us. "No need to be little ladies today! Come – eat, be merry! Look in your stockings and under the tree!" Father was so happy. I noticed that he didn't say eat, drink, and be merry. Father and Reverend Beecher are religious men most of the time, but I know that father, at least, had already imbibed a little Christmas cheer as he called it. Imbibed. That's one of my new words. I hoped I wouldn't get another dictionary. The ritual began anew: prayers, breakfast with hot cakes, syrup and scrambled eggs, Bible reading and then presents! I imitated Tiny Tim and shouted to the world, "God bless us everyone!" Charlotte, Emily, and I raced to the table. I beat and they said that's because I'm the youngest and they let me.

A log crumbled in the fireplace and made a crunching sound; embers flickered and interrupted Eugenie's dreamy reverie. For a moment or two, she really thought she was back on the prairie where Christmas was bittersweet. Family members from New York to Ohio to Kentucky and Indiana were longed for among the grown-ups. That meant that grandparents, aunts, uncles, and cousins were only known through occasional letters and pictures because they lived so far away. Such separations were especially difficult – especially for the grownups – at holiday times. The rest was fun, even when times were hard and the weather was bitterly cold.

Recalling the scenes from so many years ago was a joy. They were wonderful recordings in her brain. It was high time to retire and then rise early. Christmas Day would be so busy with the advanced drama class playing out <u>The Christmas Carol</u> for parishioners in several churches. Too, there were three families to visit. Excitement was back.

Eugenia turned off the main light, but left a small one to glow her way to her bed. A chorus of bells from the Mission Inn pealed throughout the neighborhood. It was Christmas Eve. Before reclining, Eugenie opened the small cedar chest filled with treasures on her night stand. The fragrance still faintly wafted, and that was amazing since it had been that yearned-for Christmas gift so many years ago. She decided to leave the chest open so she could capture whiffs and perhaps dream again of remembering Christmas.

Betrayal

New Year's celebration in downtown Riverside drew almost everyone in town to enjoy the promise of a prosperous 1912. Strings of electric Christmas lights still hung from store to store, and display windows featured baubles, tinsel, decorated trees, and the latest styles to ogle and purchase for the coming months. The Mission Inn, as always, was the biggest attraction, and Mr. Miller and family, as always, greeted citizens and tourists alike in welcoming everyone to lavish sights and food for the holiday season. Auld Lang Syne blared from speakers attached to Victrolas, and a citywide chorus resulted from people looking forward to goals for the new year and making resolutions that they might keep, but more likely forget about by Spring.

The night air was crisp and clear because smudge pots to maintain survivable temperatures for the citrus crops had not been fired up yet. Children raced around the streets that had been closed off to traffic, and young lovers roamed the area hand-in-hand. Eugenie, out with several friends, reminded herself how very fortunate she was to live in a town known as Paradise on Earth in spite of more cars on the streets, so much affluence that students were becoming materialistic, and many newcomers who lacked the values expected of Riversiders. Still, it was beautiful, it was home, and she was happy.

The scene changed in the next few days, and everyone was back into accustomed routines. Eugenie's life was busy. Aside from initiating several new clubs at school, she devoted hours to preparing a presentation for the Southern California Teachers Association Conference that would take up most of her Easter vacation. Several high school seniors needed letters of recommendation to send to Berkeley and Stanford. She was often too focused on her teaching and difficult administrative duties due to the double sessions to participate in her usual community activities, but she continued to work avidly with the Christian Endeavor group at church, and maintained staunch positions on American Indian Education. The first few months of the year were unusually traumatic with deaths of several friends, two serious student accidents with automobiles, and of course the sinking of the Titanic which immobilized the whole country.

In the mean time, behind the scenes, the members of the School Board took care of business. One of the members acted as secretary, and minutes of their meetings were written out by hand, but they were not circulated. They were kept in folders – just for the record. Here are samples of the minutes that came to light after school was out in June.

Minutes of Riverside City Schools Board Meeting
May 17, 1912

Mrs. Atwood introduced the following motion to wit:

"I move the adoption of the following: Notice is hereby given by this Board of Education of Riverside, to Miss Eugenie Fuller, new Principal of the Girls High School in said District that her services will not be required for the ensuing year and that the Clerk of this Board be directed to serve such notice on Miss Fuller, according to law on or before the tenth day of June, 1912."

The motion was seconded by Mr. Gage and the roll being called, the vote was as follows:

Gage voted aye
Atwood voted aye
Moulton voted no
Craig voted no
Strang voted aye

The Chair declared the motion carried.

Minutes of Riverside City Schools Board Meeting
May 22, 1912

Moved by Mrs. Atwood, seconded by Mr. Gage that the clerk be instructed to notify Miss Fuller that her services will not be required for the ensuing year. Motion discussed but not voted upon.

Mrs. Stella Atwood

Termination
May 28, 1912

Eugenie read the notice again. It didn't make sense. Ruth came in and reached for the paper. "I heard," she said, "but I want to see it with my own eyes.

"They really did it." She creased the letter and slid it back into the envelope. "What are you going to do?"

"It's incredible. Just incredible. There must be a mistake. No. No mistake. He meant it. He's destroyed me – didn't let me speak on my own behalf – didn't tell me – I had to find out by this cold announcement – what do you mean – What am I going to do? I'm ruined. Professionally, I'm ruined! I pray the traitors get justice. Not revenge – justice. That will be the worse for them. Oh, dear God!

"How can I walk out of here? How can I bear the humiliation? What did I do? Tell me, Ruth, they won't tell me – I'll ask, but with a letter like this? They won't have the courage to look me in the eye and accuse me."

Ruth knew that was true. Eugenie stopped pacing and sat in her oversized Principal's chair. Her breathing became more regular, and Ruth sat quietly and held Eugenie's hand. For minutes – nearly half an hour, they had nothing to say. Ruth was as stunned as Miss Fuller, especially since her duties were being shifted more and more to Mr. Wheelock's needs. People who had engineered this disaster had worked behind the scenes – never letting a word slip in the office, nor in the earshot of Ruth in the community of the plans to discredit Miss Fuller. Tears flowed from the two longtime friends. Something had to be done. Something had to be done. Something had to be done – but what? Eugenie withdrew her hand and caressed the ring on her third finger. The sparks of the diamonds and fire opals caught rays of the sunlight, but she didn't see the flashes. She only knew she was calling on Abraham for strength, for someone to care for her enough to be there and say, "Eugenie, it will be all right."

Yes, in past discussions, she had been mostly all right, but that's because the differences of opinion were out in the open. In those situations, she knew her opponents, and she argued her cases well. She remembered about the time she came back from her European trip and found that Mr. Wheelock had taken advantage of her year's absence to put some of his preferences and policies in place of hers. She had to work hard with the School Board to regain her leadership role; yet the long-promised goal of the appointment to Superintendent was not kept. That went to Arthur Wheelock for all practical matters, and legally in 1907, after continued lobbying on his part. As a gentleman and a scholar, he had planted the seeds years ago. He wasn't as qualified, but he got the job. No matter, she had told herself. She would still be in charge of the high school and enjoy continued happiness in working with her students.

And now, it was gone. All gone. Everything was gone.

She wanted to wait until everyone left the building before closing the office door and walking home. Ruth would have none of it. Together, they walked down the street. Ruth opened the door, turned on lights and hugged Eugenie. There was a sudden evening chill, and a swinging shutter on one of the windows made Eugenie's Hotel Reynold's apartment feel ominous. Ruth made tea for the two of them, and they sat in stunned silence. Time passed. She didn't want to leave, but Eugenie insisted. "I'll be all right. I'll see you at the regular time tomorrow. Goodnight and thank you, Ruth. You are a good friend."

Then Eugenie was alone. Should she call someone she trusted? But who, now, would that be? She needed time to search her mind for clues about what others had done or said in the last days, weeks, months. How long had this been going on? Who knew about it and said nothing? Weren't those people enemies just as well as the ones who expedited her removal? Maybe only a tight circle did know. Certainly by tomorrow's paper, everyone would know. Every part of her burned. Shame flooded her body, and she wanted to call out for help. What about the Board members who had sponsored her for so many years? How could they knuckle under to the upstarts newly elected to the Board? Who held the power now? No, she couldn't call Mr. Moulton nor Mr. Craig; not yet. Well, what about her attorney? He was out of town – attending a funeral in Galesburg. What about members of the Woman's Club, or her Presbyterian Church friends? No. What about real estate and banking people she did business with on a regular basis? Many townspeople owed her favors – some because of financial salvations and some because of personal family situations. No. Already, that sounded like bribery. She must depend on volunteers to help her. The realization hit. She had cut herself off. By always being in charge, others came to her, not the reverse. She suddenly realized that she was turning Abraham's ring on her third finger. If only he were here and could repeat his mantra, "Genie, it will be all right." Abe. Of course. She would call him, but not tonight. The hour was late in Galesburg.

Eugenie needed a little heat, even though it was late May. A few burning logs added a bit of help, but before the embers died down, sobs shook her and once they started, she couldn't pull them back. She paced the floor, she went to the door and stood on the back patio for a while, she walked from room to room, and she fell across her bed. Shame and burning heat in every cell of her body engulfed her over and over throughout the night. Breathing was irregular, and choking coughs occurred without warning. She wanted to die. She prayed over and over, but panic continued. She decided to get ready for work.

Later that week, in a letter to Emily, she recounted those dreadful hours.

"I looked in the mirror. My face was puffed. My eyes looked crazy through swollen lids. I stood there for quite awhile – and then watched my lips in the mirror as I repeated

Dear Miss Fuller,

The members of the Board have considered staff needs and have determined that your services will not be needed anymore.

This action was finalized at the Board meeting last night, May 27, 1912 and becomes effective at the close of this term, the tenth of June, 1912.

Best wishes and Kind Regards,
I remain yours truly,

Arthur N. Wheelock, Superintendent

"It was only when I recited the letter to myself and the speaking face looked back at me that the words fell like rocks on my numb head, and the tears began again. Then they wouldn't stop.

"At dawn, I bathed my face, took time with my bath, examined my swollen face and powdered myself with an extra flourish. I chose my new burgundy skirt which rustles over my petticoats and the whisper batiste blouse that would soften my anguish."

About ready to leave for school, she lectured herself in the mirror. "They want to destroy me, and indeed they have struck a mortal blow to my life and future. Very well. No – NOT very, very well! They'll see my carcass every day, and I'll be a daily reminder to them of their pettiness and vindictiveness and Christian generosity. The meanness, the hypocrites, the unfairness of it all!"

Eugenie closed the door firmly. Within a few minutes, she was walking briskly towards school. Did she acknowledge the turned heads? Note the stares? Even though people said later that they could not say, talk circulated within the hour about how still in charge she appeared, and they marveled at her control. If only she had looked pitiful, vulnerable, tearful, most would have rushed up to her. How could they when she obviously didn't need help?

"There's no need to worry about her. She's probably got an ace up her sleeve – probably has inside information on every important family in this town. She'll survive. We'll just stand aside and watch the show." The adults turned to their tasks, went their way, and Miss Fuller walked alone.

As she neared the school, students gathered toward her from all directions. Their silent gazes, their touching her hands, leaning toward her, offering to carry her books and papers, and the love reflected in their eyes and tear-stained faces made her steps falter. Her eyes blinked often as she looked down, and the tears dropped. She couldn't help it. These children were the love of her life. Then she got hold of herself, arched her back and continued to walk briskly toward the school entrance. She smiled at them and patted them back, took back her books, went into her office, closed the door and collapsed in sobs that could be heard in the hallway where students had silently gathered and where Ruth was standing.

Conversations were halting and serious. "My mom said..." began one, and "Yes, we need to do a petition..." said another. "The only way to get this settled is to go to the Board, my father said, and I am..."

"The man who has done this horrible deed is Board member _____. My folks said he campaigned on getting rid of Miss Fuller, but people laughed at him because it sounded bizarre."

Several names were mentioned that were negatively involved, and Ruth relayed them in a torrent to Miss Fuller. "There is Board member _____ who promised to remedy certain situations when he was elected, there is Stella Atwood, your nemesis at the Indian Institute, there is Mrs. _____ who claims that you let the girls get pregnant under your supervision, and people have been saying that her daughter went into Los Angeles for an abortion. There is Board member _____ who is full of it, and Mr. Wheelock, of course. People are saying that no action would have been taken without his approval, and apparently your clashes with him over the formation of a boys' high school and a girls' high school offered him a way out of the controversy."

By the end of the day, a petition signed by ninety-five per cent of the high school student body was ready for submission to the Board of Education. Several of the active PTA members accompanied student representatives to the Board President's home that evening. He accepted the petition, thanked them for their concern, and bid them good night.

"He doesn't care what we say," said _____ as they lingered on the sidewalk outside his house. His mind is made up. He's been a big supporter for years, so you can bet someone else is calling his hand. Now what do we do?"

As it turned out, not very much. Parents wrote letters to the editor of the local paper. A reporter (a former student) wrote an article about the deep respect the students had for Miss Fuller, and he expanded the article to quote former students and community admirers. The Riverside Press and The Daily Enterprise published the article without changing a word and gave the coverage coveted space on the front page of the local news.

The die was cast. The three Board members held to their position. Although Board members told their friends that they listened to everything people wanted to say, there was no formal hearing and no mention at the Board meeting about its intent because, said the President, personnel matters were not discussed in public.

After twenty-six years of laudatory service, Miss Fuller was dismissed without a cause cited – only two weeks, the Press noted, before the tenure law for teachers went into effect and only a few months before pensions were to be issued for state service. Miss Fuller had no funds from the district or state to keep her from becoming indigent. Her year's salary in 1911-1912 of $2000.00 had been paid. According to the District position, the Board and Mr. Wheelock, the Superintendent, owed her nothing.

Guilt. Guilt engulfed the city like heavy fog. For months, it hung in the air as people talked among themselves while waiting for prescriptions to be filled at the drug stores, standing in line at the banks, sitting in doctors' waiting rooms, and visiting on street corners when the town came alive on

Friday nights. Everywhere, there were muted voices, shocked comments, and expressions of guilt. It was even worse after church services on Sundays, in the Woman's Club meetings, and the men's organizations. The naysaying Board members were avoided – actually ostracized in many cases – and after several embarrassing encounters, were seldom seen at community social gatherings for weeks on end. At family evening dinners, sons and daughters eyed parents with shock and disdain for not practicing what they preached – stand up and be counted for being morally strong. It didn't stop there. Over the years, Miss Fuller had become an influential and experienced businesswoman with several properties and someone to call upon when townspeople needed financial favors. Contacting her now to request personal loans was awkward. It didn't stop there. Miss Fuller blamed herself for ignoring obvious signs of trouble and for not seeking support from the Old Guard, old timers who were the power brokers in and around Riverside who regarded her as one of their own.

What to do? Miss Fuller (as usual) led the way.

"Her heart must be breaking, but look at her. She's carrying on as if nothing happened to her."

"That's the point. I heard her telling someone that the decision to make the changes were due to other viewpoints. She said, 'I'm the identical person today that I've been for twenty-six years in this great city.'"

"Yes, and she told my husband that she will continue to work with university and state officials to recognize our students and help however she can."

"You have to give her credit."

"I'll say."

"There's talk that voting people off the Board will send a better message than people protesting at this late point.

A short time later, The Press Enterprise ran this article:

MISS EUGENIE FULLER GIVEN TOKEN OF APPRECIATION
BY GROUP OF ADMIRING FRIENDS

Miss Eugenie Fuller, principal of the girls' high school here, who is severing her connection with the Riverside public schools, has been presented with a handsome piece of silver as a token of appreciation by a group of friends who accompanied it with the following letter:

To Miss Eugenie Fuller, Riverside:

Dear Madam – On the occasion of the severance of your relations with the high school of the city of Riverside, we deem it only fit and proper that we should express to you our appreciation of the services which you have rendered the school during your association as principal and teacher with it.

You have for more than twenty years been closely identified with the Riverside high school. You have seen it grow from the small beginnings to the present size and place. We believe that it has been a marked success that has held and holds a place in the very front rank of the high schools of the state. This is the opinion of the educational experts of the state. Visiting school men have remarked upon the efficiency apparent; the fine control displayed. It is evidenced by the training shown and the work done by its graduates in universities and colleges, in normal schools, and in the varied lines of business.

We congratulate you that the alumni have always been your loyal supporters; that the boys and the girls, after they have gone out from the school and have tested, in wider fields, the results of the work done here, have recognized the value of your tuition and have returned to tell you so.

We appreciate your worth to the school, and we most heartily wish for you, in whatever place your choice may lie, the same measure of success that has attended your administration in the Riverside high school.

We herewith present to you a token, to demonstrate in a small way the respect which we entertain for you.

Yours very truly,

Lyman Evans, S. C. Evans, W. A. Purington, Stanley J. Castleman, W. G. Irving, Hugh H. Craig, E. S. Moulton.

(note: These men were all School Board members during Miss Fuller's service in the school district.)

The date is missing from the accompanying article, too, but the following unedited scrapbook's clipping was beside the one above.

SCHOOL ALUMNI PRAISE MISS FULLER
Resolutions of Appreciation on Principal at the Girls' High School Adopted at Business Meeting of Former Students Held Last Evening

At the business meeting of the high school alumni held last night, it was moved by E. V. Seares and seconded by Ethelbert Dole, that the following resolutions be adopted, a copy to be sent to Miss Eugenie Fuller, that a copy be sent to each of the daily papers, and that a copy be spread upon the minutes of this meeting. The motion was unanimously carried.

"Whereas the board of education of the city of Riverside has seen fit to remove Miss Fuller as principal of the girls' high school of the city of Riverside, without assigning any reasons therefore, or preferring any charges against her, or commending in any way her many years of service in the public schools of this city; and,

"Whereas the character of her work and influence among the students is sufficiently shown by the standing of the graduates in universities and colleges throughout the land, her own position among the educators in this state, and the place occupied by the Riverside high school among the schools of the state,

"Now, therefore, be it resolved by the alumni of the Riverside high school that while we acknowledge the authority and control of the board of education in all matters relative to the public schools of this city, and as a body believe in upholding all regular constituted authority,

"Nevertheless, Be it further resolved, that an injustice which may have been unintentional has been done to Miss Fuller, in that she has been removed without assigning any reasons therefor, or preferring any charges against her, or commending in any way her many years of service in the public schools of this city, or for her assistance in placing the Riverside high schools in their present high position among the schools and with the educators of this state; and,

"Be it further resolved that the alumni do hereby express their confidence in Miss Fuller, not only for the actual teaching done by her in the schools, but for her assistance in other ways to the alumni while students in the schools; and,

"Be it further resolved, that the alumni do hereby give great credit to Miss Fuller for her work and services in placing the Riverside high school in its present notable position among the high schools of the state; and,

"Be it further resolved, that we would deprecate such summary action in the case of any person who has filled a public office and has shown by his or her work their fitness to fill such a position."

Minutes of Riverside City Schools Board Meeting
July 26, 1912

Superintendent Wheelock recommended the following teachers for appointment (seven listed on record), and Jas. Winne, Principal Girls High School.

Moved by Mrs. Atwood, and seconded by Mr. Gage, that the recommendations be accepted. On roll call the following vote resulted:

Mr. Gage voted aye, except for the teachers recommended

Mrs. Atwood voted aye, except for the teachers recommended

Mr. Moulton voted aye, except for the principal recommended

Mr. Craig voted aye except for the principal recommended

The vote being a tie, the Chair declared the motion lost.

Up until now, few citizens, if any, had requested to see the routine minutes of the Riverside City Schools Board Meetings. The desire – even need – for scrutiny of the School Board's activities changed with the May decisions that caught people unaware. Citizens began to ask questions and got few answers. A news reporter asked to see the Board Minutes, a public document, and realized that numerous decisions had been made recently and implemented without full dissemination of the facts to the community.

In the past, so much had been done on trust and with little questioning, including the Board's frequent request for additional tax revenues over the years, mainly because Riversiders vigorously lauded educational endeavors and had been happy to financially support their fine schools. The new Polytechnic High School for the boys was the latest example.

No more. News reporters not only asked to review the Board minutes, they began to attend meetings and sit completely through each agenda's minutia. Even though they were not privy to personnel matters that were held behind closed doors, their very presence in the meeting room set a tone that the community was watching and would no longer brook the type of secrecy that had surrounded Miss Fuller's career demise.

Rumors had floated recently about the appointment of Mr. Winne to assume the principalship of the Girls High School, and the community was abuzz with how the Board members would likely vote. The appointment of the seven elementary and high school teachers was not the issue. How the members of the School Board would vote on Miss Fuller's successor was of vital interest.

On July 26, the final decision had to be postponed to another meeting. The School Board members were now fully aware that they were being watched, listened to, and scrutinized. A strong sentiment against some of the members was evolving. Interestingly, someone went so far as to copy the minutes of the July 26 meeting pertaining to Mr. Winne and posted it publicly on windows of several businesses in town.

Adjusting

"What to do? Well, I'm not leaving. Instead, buying a permanent home is a good idea. It's been pleasant living at the Hotel Reynolds for the last two years or so – especially when I have my own apartment and go only a few steps for delicious culinary pleasures. It's been convenient to live downtown – the business hub with the Courthouse, the stores, and active life and, of course, being so close to school has been a blessing – but I'm shut out of that now – well, the school, anyway. What to do with my time – indeed, with my life?

"Riverside is home and I'll certainly continue on here. And what will I do? Conduct my real estate transactions, oversee other financial interests – perhaps add to my properties downtown, and renovate my brick building on Main and Tenth. I've had several requests lately about maintenance, and I'll take care of those tasks post-haste. Of course, I'll advise and help any former students who consult me and will welcome their friends, too. And maintain my contacts with Berkeley and Stanford. My writing projects have been on the shelves way too long, and now I must quit procrastinating about completing them. Then there is my church, the Woman's Club, the activities at the Inn with the Millers, and my other dear friends, along with the students I've fostered for years. There's travel, perhaps, although there's no place else I want to be right now. My gracious, I'll be ever so busy.

"My nemeses may think I'll slink away, but people who really know me shrug, just as I do. They know better. Yes, I shall buy a home. A really interesting one on a quiet street and close to downtown. And I know just the house to consider. Tomorrow, I'll make some inquiries."

Miss Fuller's slow, ponderous steps evolved to a professional stride as she talked to herself, and she walked briskly for more than an hour. The click of her heels on the pavement spoke confidence, her shoulders arched back, and her chin moved upward with a determined tilt. She smiled and exchanged pleasantries with others. One businessman commented to his wife a bit later, "That Miss Fuller. Never was there such a lady of spunk and honesty. Those scoundrels have no idea that they're finished in this town if she continues to live here, and she will! My, oh, my. Such a distinguished lady of paramount importance!" His words were prophetic.

The dissenting School Board members and their loyal constituents grumbled that wherever they went – shopping for groceries, banking, purchasing tools, paying on accounts, going to church services, cheering the local sports, attending events at the Loring Theatre – Miss Fuller was there, and looked directly at them before continuing on her way. Townspeople showed her deep respect and admiration, and some openly repudiated those who had ended her career. Even the Superintendent felt the sting of criticism, although it was seldom voiced in his presence. Why didn't she fade into the background or just go away? Wasn't that what a woman terminated from her position should do? Soon there was talk around town about recalling some Board members and by the next election, it happened. Perhaps it was the only way that the community could show support and do justice.

Miss Fuller was soon quite comfortable in her new surroundings except for having to do her own cooking when she just didn't feel like making the trek to eat out. Like everything else she attempted, she became adept. Recalling long forgotten recipes from her years on the farm, her larder was soon filled, and her dinners for her social groups became coveted.

Large tortoise-shell colored cats – Odysseus and Penelope – became household companions almost immediately. A neighbor, in preparing to knock at Miss Fuller's door one day, overheard her comments of a historical nature. The visitor was amused to hear meows in response. "And that's why your names are Odysseus and Penelope," Miss Fuller said to them before responding to her guest.

Miss Fuller and her neighbors enjoyed casual conversations, and they visited frequently – usually in the mid-morning hours and in the coolness of the late afternoons. Working with plants in their front yards, greeting passersby from the front porch swings, and complimentary remarks about the beautiful, exotic flowers in nearly every yard gave the impetus for discussing the weather, the latest events detailed in the newspaper, and apolitical comments. Decorum ruled; political and religious comments were avoided and saved for social groups of like mind. All in all, the experience of home ownership was a delight.

Miss Fuller tried to be near the sidewalk tending her flowers when students walked by at regular times. Her passion for inspiring young people never flagged. One such person was Edmund Yeager, a neighbor who lived in the stone and concrete house just up the block and next street over. His front yard sported all kinds of cacti – from ground huggers to tree-like specimens. Two kinds of palm and a Joshua tree were featured. It was a bit of desert surrounded by a fertile oasis.

"Young Mr. Yeager is such a pleasant person. It's about time for him to be passing by, so I think I'll go trim my roses and ask him how he's doing in his college classes. He is such an inspiration." Sure enough, Eugenie had no more than reached her customary spot than he appeared at the end of the block, loaded down as usual with his books. He saw her from afar and hastened his step. The inspiration was mutual. They had another bond. It was he who had convinced her to adopt Odysseus and Penelope – two kittens from the same litter that were placed anonymously on his parent's doorstep. "You would be doing us a huge favor and perhaps one for yourself, too. If you find them impossible, I'll retrieve them." How could she negate his plea? Because he was such a decent person in the finest sense of the word and totally dedicated to his studies, she agreed. How very fortunate, she thought repeatedly as she watched their antics and enjoyed their company.

The young scientist and his mentor conversed frequently about his class choices and his aims in life. He wanted to study the desert, he said.

And not only the desert, but the flora and fauna throughout the area. He was enthusiastic and determined, and she firmly encouraged him, but one day her frustration emerged when she said, "Edmund, be careful. The world is not always what we hope for. Be careful. You give the world the best that you have, and the worst will come back to you. I predict, though, that your love for plants and animals will put you in good stead. They are more trustworthy than people."

Miss Fuller's Residence: 4187 Seventh Street
also known as 1187 for years prior to town's expansion and renumbering

Abraham's Goodbye
May 26, 1915

No sound. The house was quiet. Eerily so. And lonely. A tree branch brushed against an upstairs window and sounded both stealthy and gentle at the same time. Like an intruder moving carefully.

Eugenie crisscrossed the papers she had been studying – separating the audited ones from the ones still to be done, aligned the edges just so, closed a book or two that she had consulted just to make sure her financial assessments had been accurate, adjusted the kerosene light that she was still accustomed to using, and carefully moved the lamp to the center of the table.

It was too early to go to bed and she didn't feel like reading. What else could she do? No, she didn't want to make a supper, but a cup of hot tea sounded good. She spooned loose, black leaves into the small, brown teapot that used to belong to her mother, and before that to her mother, heated some water in a small teakettle and soon had a satisfying brew. She turned down the wick of the kitchen lamp and sat in near darkness at the kitchen table. Near darkness. A small, lighted lamp in the parlor allowed for safe passage through the house and made soft shadows on the walls. The lamp was sturdy and portable and so Eugenie routinely carried it upstairs when she retired for the night and placed it back on the table the next morning. There it was – waiting for its journey. Instead, Eugenie put both elbows on the table and nursed the hot cup of tea in her hands.

Something was wrong. She knew inside her that something was terribly wrong. What could it be? Had one of her railroad stock investments dived, would Herbert Thornton default on his loan payment again, was her nemesis fencing her in with personal denigrations again? Nothing seemed to be the answer. Eugenie poured another cup of tea. She closed her eyes as she sipped, set the cup back into its saucer and was about to get up

180

when the message hit. "Something has happened to Abraham." Deep within her, she knew the truth. It was as if he had told her himself. It was as if he were beside her for moments on end. They had promised each other years ago that they would contact each other when it was time to say goodbye. She felt a body near her chair, felt a faint breeze on her forehead and knew that Abraham had kept his word.

Morning light streamed through the kitchen window. Eugenie still sat at the table with an empty teacup and after staring at her hands shredding the fringe on the napkin she had grasped, she moaned, wept, sobbed at the hand she had dealt herself and the gap in her life without him. The sun caught a sharp glint on her ring, and she twisted it around her finger. Around and around. Two fire opals surrounded by three diamonds. It was such a beautiful ring. She had worn it since he placed it on her finger, and they pledged that even though they were not together, they would never be apart. That had always been true – since they were teenagers on their adjoining farms in North Henderson – and even when they vehemently disagreed and parted ways from time to time.

She had just moved to the parlor to snuff the light still burning and wasting oil in daylight when the phone rang. The operator connected her to her sister Em in Galesburg, Illinois, who confirmed what Eugenie already knew. Abraham had died last night. "About 11:30 your time?" asked Eugenie.

"Yes," Em said. "He was sitting up in bed, reading a book, and his heart failed. What made you say 11:30?"

"He stopped to say goodbye."

Abraham Brown

Nannie's Call
May 27, 1915

The second phone call that came at eight that morning intensified her angst. Abe had a stroke sometime after eleven last night. He had been reading in bed and when his sister Nannie checked on him at eleven-thirty, he was still wearing his glasses and his fingers separated the pages 78-79 of Browning's poems. Nan said papers and books were scattered about the bed in a disarray that showed he'd been resting and reading for his customary couple of hours in the late evening.

"Will you be coming home, Genie?"

"Yes, Nan. It's too little and too late, but how can I not be there. Page 78 was our song to each other, you know."

"Yes, I've heard it many times while he was gazing at your portrait and reciting it verbatim."

———————————————

Phone calls and visits had to be made – first to the train station for a reservation and then to her neighbor to ask her to care for Odysseus and Penelope, the tortie cats, and watch the house. Oh, and the iceman and the broker and her tenants. She scarcely had time to pack a few things when the cabbie arrived. It was John ___ and he voiced surprise that she was actually going to get into an automobile, something she had emphatically vowed never to do. What happened? She told him that a dear friend of many years had died, and she was going to the funeral in Illinois. Her head hurt and her mouth seemed full of sticky, raw cotton and tasted of blood. The angst showed in her face and demeanor. He knew better than to inquire more. He drove more carefully than usual, parked the car, and escorted her to the stationmaster.

She pressed him to take her fare, but he refused. As they parted, he looked straight at her. "Miss Fuller, you always told us that death can be a new beginning, and that our memories keep a loved one alive, and that remembering keeps the love immortal."

"Yes – you're right. I must remember my own counsel. You are wise and sensitive, John. Thank you. Truly, I thank you, and John, give my regards to your mother, an admirable woman who has remarkable children." The whistle sounded, and the conductor assisted her into the coach.

"John, such a nice young man. There he is, still waiting for the train to depart." They waved. "Too bad he didn't go on to Berkeley. When I get back, I'll call him to come visit me and see what I can do. I remember having his father, Myron, in class, too. Such a straight backed and proud person. John's a carbon copy."

The train began to move, and Eugenie settled back into the gray-ribbed, upholstered seat. The seat opposite was empty, but the occupant might be in the dining car. It was good not to have to acknowledge anyone for a bit. The seats seemed to be small these days. Not as comfortable as she remembered on her last trip to Galesburg. Remember, Remember, Remember – the wheels clacked the word out rhythmically. The dreaded moment had arrived. The phone calls and packing and talking were over. And now the memories came tumbling forward, then receding to let other images impress. To bring a sense of calmness, she tried to dwell on one incident at a time and force herself to bring closure and say goodbye to it before she went on to another. The one she favored most at the moment was sitting in an early fall haystack with Abe, enjoying the full harvest moon, the fragrant new mown grass, and each other as couples square danced near by. She pulled herself erect, crossed her ankles and tried to convey the idea that she was in charge and not allow the world to see the total chaos within. She pulled a weathered book from her satchel and opened it to page 78 – not that she needed it for the tender words, but to prevent stares from strangers as she let the message roll from her lips.

Life In A Love

Escape me?
Never--
Beloved!
While I am I, and you are you,
So long as the world contains us both,
Me the loving and you the loth
While the one eludes, must the other pursue.
My life is a fault at last, I fear:
It seems too much like a fate, indeed!
Though I do my best I shall scarce succeed.
But what if I fail of my purpose here?
It is but to keep the nerves at strain,
To dry one's eyes and laugh at a fall,
And, baffled, get up and begin again,--
So the chase takes up one's life, that's all.
While, look but once from your farthest bound
At me so deep in the dust and dark,
No sooner the old hope goes to ground
Than a new one, straight to the self-same mark,
I shape me--
Ever
Removed!

Robert Browning, of course.

She would write her own poem: What Might Have Been Will Never Be. First though, she would dedicate it to him. "It's easier to write facts than emotions right now," she thought.

Beloved
Abraham Miller Brown
October 4,1846 – May 26, 1915

1870 – 1875 Teacher
1875 – 1915 Lawyer and Illinois State Senator

**Abraham Brown (as were his kin)
was buried in the Fuller Family Cemetery**

Important Visitors

A very large, burnished leather, maroon-hued scrapbook lay in the display window of a Dickens-like bookstore and bindery in London. Eugenie crimped her lips, a developing habit, as she mentally tried to fit the possible purchase into her travel trunk. The book was frightfully expensive, made by hand, and the word Scrapbook was written in Spencerian script and etched in gold leaf. It was a beauty and an exquisite cache for the many clippings she had collected over the years – clippings marking the career journeys of her students. This book would do them proud. "Yes, even if it won't fit into my trunk, I really must have it." Fit, it did, though, along with heavy brown wrapping covering the treasure twice. The bookmeister, besides the pounds in cost, felt well paid just by observing the pleasure it was giving the buyer. She must indeed be a rare caring person to want to honor her students' successes, he thought to himself after engaging her in conversation. He unrolled more butcher wrap to insure proper protection.

Following her exciting sojourn in Europe and her return to her duties as Principal at the Riverside High School, the elegant scrapbook was ensconced on a table near the book-borrowing counter in the school library. It was a magnet to visitors. When students returned to visit Miss Fuller and other teachers, they saw their own exploits on display and were especially glad to read about their classmates. It had been a fortunate, whimsical purchase, she thought often, and she had made a choice decision in buying it. Now it reposed in her foyer – on top of the worn but seaworthy trunk that had accompanied her so many places since having to leave the school. Showing only a little age, the leather scrapbook was a featured welcome for guests who entered her home. It was a special treasure.

On a particularly cloudy, blustery – about to pour buckets – day, she thought lightening her spirits by reviewing the clippings was a good plan. Placing the tome on the dining room table, she opened it to a random spot. "Aaah, now look at that large news clipping of President Theodore Roosevelt planting the orange tree at the Mission Inn, surrounded by prestigious citizens along with students representing every school in the city. At the dinner celebration the night before, high school girls carrying long-stemmed bouquets of flowers enveloped in colorful tissue presented them to the President of the United States. Behind each girl stood a young man in his best suit – all there to honor the important visitor. The Riverside Press had produced a large photograph suitable for framing, and it fit nicely on the center of the page. Each high school student participating in the special occasion had autographed the page. "Very nice. Excellent," she murmured.

Eugenie had arranged for a student representative and his family to sit at one of the Education Tables at The Glenwood Mission Inn and do the school's honors on her behalf. She did not want to draw attention to herself, especially since she knew Mr. Roosevelt from other social encounters. That gesture failed, however, when the President spoke enthusiastically of the Riverside High School's fine reputation and then walked over, presented an engraved card to Miss Fuller, and encouraged cheers. And there it was with his personal greeting on its own special page in the book.

She turned to other clippings of presidential visits to Riverside. Preparing for their appearances provided exciting opportunities to study current events, United States History, even political parties, and permission for students to be part of the welcoming presentations was honored. The teachers at all grade levels stressed appropriate behavior, respect, and proper etiquette. Parents talked with pride about their children's involvement in the opportunity of a lifetime to see the President of the United States. The Mission Inn, historically called the Glenwood Hotel and other names before that, full of beauty and in the heart of downtown, hosted the guests, partly because of its spacious setting and renowned graciousness, and partly because the Inn was owned by Mr. Frank Miller, a most influential and generous townsman who had early on developed his father's adobe cottages bit by bit into an exotic destination for travelers. He wanted the children involved, so classes were rotated to enable many students to share in the glory of meeting important people. Because of time and space limitations, students who missed seeing one President or other celebrated visitor were placed first on the list for the next important visitor. The High School was always represented by students who presented flowers, gifts, welcoming songs, and orchestral music.

"Let's see. How many Presidents were there?" There was no need for the question – even to herself. The events were etched in her brain, and the clippings only emphasized the occasions. "Benjamin Harrison on April 23, 1891, William McKinley ever so briefly and without any fanfare in 1901, Theodore Roosevelt twice – May 7, 1903 and again in 1911 – and William Howard Taft on October 12, 1909. We had to share our visitors with the nearby rival city of Redlands, and we even shared the custom-built chair for Mr. Taft's comfort," she mused to herself. "The only faux pas I can remember about his visit was when one of the tykes in elementary school said to another in a loud voice, 'Lookee, there he is, and is he ever fat!' President Taft heard it, of course, smiled affably at the lad and said, 'You have a keen eye, my son!' Everyone chuckled, and at that moment, high school girls lay armfuls of roses at his feet while a trio of violinists serenaded him."

The weather had cleared. Sunshine streamed over the aging pages. Eugenie closed the book to protect them from the glare and then carried her treasure back to its spot in the foyer. She opened the back door for fresh air now that the wind had subsided and was struck by the large cumulus clouds against the backdrop of a blue sky.

"I'll sit out here in the yard for a spell and pretend my mother and I are looking for cloud pictures." There they were, wafting gently in the sky. "Mama favored finding pictures of farm animals, especially of horses' heads. I'll find some for her." Her memories of those long ago pleasures were bittersweet, one especially. She finally had some time alone with her mother because her sisters were visiting friends. They lay in tall meadow grass, along with Brownie, and spent hours talking with each other and looking for cloud pictures. Brownie suddenly barked and rain clouds, too, warned them to scurry. They ran helter-skelter towards the house as thunder roared and big raindrops pelted them. It was a perfect day.

The SPOTLIGHT

Vol. 2 No. 14   Riverside, California, Thursday, Jan. 12, 1922   Price 5 Cents

Friday Jan. 13, Elks Club

CO-EDUCATION IS ADOPTED

PADDOCK STATES TWO FACTORS IN GOOD ATHLETICS

World Famed Sprinter Says Condition and Sportsmanship Only Factors

PADDOCK ADDRESSES HI-Y

Big Crowd at Spirited meeting in Honor of Charles Paddock: Gives Fine Talk

Charles W. Paddock, world's fastest sprinter, holder of seven world's records, and without doubt the fastest man in ancient, mediaeval and modern history, last Tuesday evening delivered the most stirring and interesting talk ever presented before the Hi-Y Club of Riverside. His subject was, "Condition Counts." Some 150 members and guests heard this unusual talk.

Paddock gave interesting illustrations including the races at the

CHARLES PADDOCK GIVES INTERVIEW TO SPOTLIGHT REPORTER

Mentions "Jud" House Of Poly; Impresses Value Of Condition

By
Russell Waite

"What Riverside High School needs in the way of athletics is another "Jud" House, declared Charles Paddock, world's champion sprinter of all times, in an interview with a representative of the Spotlight Tuesday night. He is a good example of one keeping in condition. Everyone remembers "Jud" House, the famous hurdler from Poly who took third place in the hurdles of the Olympic games. Mr. Paddock knows him well and pays him a fine tribute.

Speaking of Riverside in general he stated that it was a very nice place and that he enjoyed his time here very much. He said he had never seen the High School and didn't know much about Poly, but had heard a good deal about the accomplishments.

GIRLS AND BOYS SCHOOLS TO BE COMBINED SOON

Resolution of Board of Education Authorizes Formation of Plans, Unanimous.

NEARLY TWELVE YEARS

Board To call Special Meeting To Plan change To Take Place in Near Future

At the last meeting of the new Board of Education held last Monday night a resolution was adopted approving Co-Education in the Riverside High Schools and Junior College. The resolution called for a completion of plans for the carrying out of the project. The resolution was adopted without a vote against it.

Mr. W. T. Desmond of the old Board introduced the resolution at the meeting of the Board on December ... referred

GIRLS HIGH PLAYS FIRST BASKETBALL GAME AT SANTA ANA

Defeat Santa Ana Girls By Score Of 31-7; Santa Ana's First Girls Game

Riverside Girls High School completely outclassed the Santa Ana girls six when they defeated the latter on their ground.

Friday afternoon the Riverside Girl's High school completely outclassed the Santa Ana girls in the first interscholastic game they have played this season when they downed the opponents by a score of 31 to 7.

The local girls kept up a continuous stream of baskets from the beginning of the game and from the playing witnessed there should be no doubt as to the success of the team in the season which has just opened. Although this is the Santa Ana team's first year at basketball nevertheless the G. H. S. six were kept pretty busy. They are to be commended on their team and the remarkable spirit shown during the game.

The team that journeyed to the neighboring city is as follows:

Santa Ana Forwards J. Cruik-

RIVERSIDE TOPS SCORE IN POMONA GAME FRIDAY

Hodgson, Dales, Fouch, Coffey and Roblee Outplay Opponents in Big Game

GAME ENDED SCORE 29-2

Second Citrus Belt League Game Goes To Riverside; Berdoo and Riverside Lead

BY CLAY HARNOIS

Riverside won the second game of the C. B. L. schedule last Friday on the Sherman Institute gym floor from Pomona 29-20. At the same time San Bernardino was winning their game with Redlands. The games leave Riverside and San Bernardino at the head of the list with two games won and none lost.

Thursday, January 12, 1922

Riverside High School boys and girls, segregated by the School Board and Superintendent in 1912, celebrated the announcement that co-education would be re-established in Riverside High School. Long, raucous protests by students through the years, including marches in the streets, and philosophical changes of the majority of parents led to the decision in 1922.

The Interview
1922

"Thank you so very much for granting this interview," the Riverside Press reporter said when Miss Fuller answered his knock on the door and invited him inside.

"Mr. Patton, you are welcome. It's my pleasure to see you again, and I hope I can be helpful to you. There's not much to report about me these days, but let's see what you can do. Just be factual – and I hope a little kind. Before we begin, come have a refreshment with me and tell me about what you have been doing for the last few years. I'm fully aware of your talents because I read your weekly articles in the paper, and you sound like a person of good training and character. There, take another cookie. I made plenty."

Gerald did just that, and gave Miss Fuller a brief run down on his career. He wanted to get on with the interview, though, so looking at his list of questions, he began.

"You've just come back from another trip to the Philippines. What do you find so fascinating about the islands?"

"It's not the islands, so much, although everything is beautiful there except for the heavy rains during the monsoon season. I find the people fascinating, particularly the several young men I sponsored when they were teenagers. Caring for others and eagerness to learn is part of their culture."

"You brought some students to California over the years and sent them on to the State University and Stanford, I heard."

"Yes, and helping those students were my special deeds in life."

"Are you planning any more adventures in the next year or two?"

"Probably not. I've had my fill of traveling for a while except for taking the train back to Galesburg to keep up with relatives and friends and family reunions."

"My main reason to ask for this interview is about how you reacted when you read that the high school students are going back to a co-education program. When the girls and boys were segregated into two high school programs in 1912, you were very opposed to the idea, and you retired soon after that. Do you feel vindicated now that the classes will be co-educational again? Here is a clipping about it from the paper."

"Thank you. I read the article from the Poly Spotlight student paper, as well as from the Press, and wanted to leap for joy and do a handspring or two. Many students have protested the absurd policy from the beginning. Perhaps the most publicized rebellion involved their street protests about mandatory vaccines – which really wasn't about the vaccines – but a ploy. At long last, a great wrong to our young people has been corrected. Diluting the academic programs and separating the girls from the boys was a fiasco and travesty. It's good to know that the citizens and Board of Education have realized the mistake and are correcting it."

"Mr. Wheelock, the Superintendent, now favors the change, too."

"Yes, so I've heard."

"Miss Fuller, aside from learning about your travels and your reaction to making the high school co-educational again, I have some questions to ask you about your last years at the high school. Do you mind talking about it?"

"Only if you will let me read the article before it goes to print, reason being – I do not want to rattle people's feelings, hurt anyone, or promote animosity. Life's too short for that. Yet, I'd like to talk to you about it because my story may help others who find themselves in the same difficult situation. There have been times when I've wanted to counsel individuals about the signs that I see affecting their careers, and would have if I had been asked. That whole situation is one that still deeply troubles me."

"How so?"

"I didn't see it coming. And I should have. Looking back on it, the signs were screaming at me."

"And the signs were?"

"Ah, you are getting better and better in this interview. Kudos."

"Thanks, but I wasn't thinking to ask because I'm a reporter. I just want to hear your story."

"Then you're going to be a great journalist. Listen. Listen to the stories – what's said and what's omitted. Delve through the anguish, beyond reasons and excuses until you reach the kernels of truth. Discernment is a great teacher, requiring reflection and inner searching. It leads to wisdom and fosters honest, unvarnished judgments. In my case, there were several strands of happenings that braided themselves into a life-altering story. Let me explain.

"There were few parties and no dances at our school, partly because Riverside was a strong church town from the settlement's beginning, and partly because I simply would not brook them. The Board of Education, all through the years, established restraints on activities such as students using tobacco, liquor, and frequenting billiard rooms, and I fully supported those decisions. True, there were some wild parties in the community, and vandalism and bullying sometimes occurred, but never, never at school.

"There were other kinds of discipline problems. Some of the boys were very rambunctious and took great joy in frightening the girls just for the fun of it. Of course, the girls told their parents and the parents told me, in no uncertain terms, I remember, that it was all due to my lack of discipline. Bosh! None of that was true. They really knew that I would not have allowed unruly behavior for a minute.

"By the end of the first decade in the 1900s, times were changing rapidly. Many residents had become affluent from the citrus crops and that spurred affluence in other segments of town. Their children had more money to spend without being held accountable, less supervision of their activities outside of school – even the elementary schools – and the automobile, a cursed invention, began to outnumber horses for transportation. Could I have stopped the activities in the community? Of course not, but I certainly held sway at school. Still, I did not realize at the time the extent that I was being held accountable by some people for every difficulty high school students experienced, including intimate relationships among the teens. I had a reputation for demanding moral behavior, and I thought parents certainly knew that the actions of some of the students were not due to character flaws within myself. I was wrong. So that was one strand.

"Mr. Wheelock and I had strongly divergent views on a number of issues affecting our students, and he expressed them formally throughout the community. That was not my style. I expected people to understand my philosophy of educating young people primarily through the results of seeing these fine young men and women succeed in school and graduate with sterling character. The results spoke for themselves.

"I employed Mr. Wheelock, you know – to teach history. And he did fine work and was reliable. So much so, that I mentored him to serve in my stead when I planned to take a year's leave for a wonderful trip to Europe in 1903. We locked horns when I returned a year later and saw that he had made a number of changes that did not meet my approval. I reined in some of them. The handwriting was on the wall. The strong support I had always had with the Board reversed as his grew. The Board had specified several years ago that I was to be elevated to the superintendency as soon as the city charter was approved to legally allow the position. Meanwhile, Mr. Wheelock's assignments to supervise the elementary schools and to lobby influential groups on behalf of the growing school system took him from the classroom to administrative duties delegated by the Board. In a way, I didn't care because I loved my classroom work which I could continue to do in addition to being Principal.

"What I didn't foresee was the extent to which the Board gave up their authority over hiring teachers and deciding curriculum issues by giving him carte blanche in those areas and more. We desperately needed an additional high school to house the burgeoning enrollments. On that, we teamed together until I learned that he wanted to house the boys at the new school and leave the girls at 9th and Lime. Why?

"Horrifying was his plan to institute a manual arts program strictly for the boys and to have classes for the girls to teach them to be womanly. I had taken great pride in seeing that the men graduating from Riverside High School were eligible to go on to universities without question, if they chose. While the girls were not barred from higher education, many found it difficult to enter professional fields because – can you believe it – women did not have the right to vote and to participate fully in establishing careers.

"Mr. Wheelock and I battled, and it became public knowledge. That caused citizens to take sides and watch the action. Not a good idea. It pits one against the other. Someone will lose.

"The most important strand, probably, involved the changes in the structure of the Board. As you may have read, Mr. E. W. Holmes at one time handled all the educational issues. Later, Dr. Deere and Mr. Purington helped to form the high school district. The Evans families served in the early 1900s, along with Mr. Castleman, Mr. Irving, Mr. Moulton, Mr. Craig, and Mrs. Atwood. The changes on the Board that ended my career – in the same election as the right for women to vote in California – occurred in 1911, and the power shifted. That's what I didn't see coming. Let me emphasize, Gerald, the importance of being mentored – sponsored – by those who are higher in authority than you. If you get nothing else from this interview, be aware that you cannot soar indefinitely by yourself without recognition and support of others, and those others have to feel rewarded for supporting you. If I had opened myself more to parents, their support may have pressured members of the Board. I was too proud. I thought my **results** with the **students** were all that mattered. My main support was my students, and they had no power. I wish Arthur – Mr. Wheelock – had been more loyal or that he had leveled with me. The most difficult issue for me to overcome was that people worked behind my back, and when I needed support from my colleagues, there was only silence.

"And so you know what happened in 1912. Otherwise, you would not have been so timid in asking about that time in my life. Now let's go on."

"People around town speak of you with awe as being the best teacher in the world. They say that you asked questions that required explanations – no yes or no answers would do. Also, several times I've heard that you had a devilish sense of humor that students had to think about and absorb. One comment I've heard over and over is, 'Haven't I told you a million times not to exaggerate?' What a great way to teach hyperbole!"

"Mr. Patton, encouraging students to give serious thought to solving problems, understanding historical and current issues of the times, and leading energetic, balanced lives were teaching goals that I inherited from my teachers and that I had a passion to promote. You're right. I did not condone surface answers. And, yes, I had great fun with my students. Levity is often an effective teaching tool."

"Last questions. What has given you the most joy in your life, and what do you regret?"

"My goodness. You are reaching into my soul. What has given me the most joy? That one is easy. Seeing my students enjoying their careers, some of them after great struggles in their early lives. I could name hundreds. Mr. Holmes, one of Riverside's most important leaders and member of the School Board for many years, noted 674 in one of his accounts. Come back again sometime soon, and I'll show you clippings in that large scrapbook on the trunk in the entryway. Reading about them in the daily news gives me great joy, and their letters to me are treasures. I've kept them all.

"Now. What do I regret? It's not regrets as much as 'what ifs,' and that's a dangerous place to go, a slippery slope. How do any of us know if we had taken one path instead of another that we would be more satisfied with the result?

"I think of my mother who stayed on the farm long after my father died. I didn't get to see her very often because I had chosen to live in Riverside. In her later years, she was chronically ill and could barely walk. I know she missed me terribly. Of course, one of my sisters was nearby, and her brothers and other relatives lived in town, too. For several years, she lived with Uncle Nick, her brother, and then moved in with my sister, Emily, when she retired. Still...

"I had to make a choice between getting married to the love of my life or stay single in order to teach, also a love of my life. No questions about that, please.

"Coming to Riverside was the fulfillment of a dream, and I've loved it here. That choice meant that I left Galesburg and my many friends and a comfortable life. So you see, when we do 'what ifs' – regrets, so to speak, we're led into gloominess and frustration. I have used Lady Macbeth's 'What's done cannot be undone' often as a way of moving on.

"My, my, speaking of moving on, you have extended your time and must be getting back to your other duties. I've rambled on so, but I do hope you can get a story out of all this. I do hope and expect that you will let me see your draft – not for me to correct or change, but as I said, I want it to be accurate and not hurtful to anyone."

"Including Mr. Wheelock and the Board members at the time?"

"Yes. What's done cannot be undone."

"Thank you so much for permitting the interview. I hope to do our conversation justice."

"You will. Now let me accompany you to the door."

Thinking about how he would write up the interview, Gerald Patton got into his Ford and headed back to the office. He would need to do two articles; one to give Miss Fuller's adulation for the co-education plans, and the other to step back in time and write an eye-opening analysis about the need for sponsorship. Maybe a third to honor her influence on Riverside students. He patted the steering wheel. "Yes, I know she didn't want to give you the time of day," he said to his flivver, "but forget that. In other ways, she was a woman way ahead of her time." He promised himself that he'd get back to her with drafts and ask to go over some of the stories in that big leather scrapbook in the hallway.

Who Visited Miss Fuller?
1920s

A shiny, black Cartercar pulled up to the curb on Seventh Street, and the engine continued to chug for a few minutes. The neighbors were agog. Cars on the street were not that common, and seldom in front of Miss Fuller's house. Local townspeople who visited her usually walked. Everyone knew how agitated she became around cars, and she was adamant in saying that she had ridden in one only in a desperate circumstance and never would again because they were likely to get out of control and injure someone. She sometimes recalled an experience she had on a visit back in Galesburg when an automobile out of control spooked her horse pulling a surrey. She was careened down the street until the surrey bumped into a railroad car that was stopped on the tracks. Maggie Lee, her frightened roan, was injured, but not desperately so. The scrapes where the blinders were crushed against her face took weeks to heal, and the roan pattern disappeared around the scars.

So as curtains were pulled back from the windows, the peepers were fascinated to see a young man get out of the car, check his note, retrieve a bag from behind the seat, and proceed across the sidewalk and up the steps to Miss Fuller's door. Almost immediately, the door opened as if Miss Fuller was expecting him, and the gossip traveled up and down the street and across town for those who had telephones.

"Who could it be? He isn't local, that's for sure."

"There's a decal on the window: Boalt Hall – Berkeley Law."

"What does the license plate say?"

"A California plate with a San Francisco frame!"

Was he a former student? Was he related? The son of a friend? The malcontents didn't stop there. Maybe a son from a long ago liaison? Tongues wagged, but no one had the temerity to ask outright, and Miss Fuller never mentioned the matter.

Hard Times
1930

The stock market had crashed. Every household was rocked by the financial crisis. Survival and just getting by were the baseline goals for everyone. Fears of going to the poorhouse were now serious and often on the lips of those who had struggled and saved for years to avoid that final residence. There was a time when people had made references about the county poor farm or the poor house almost in jest if things were not going their way. Now, things were not going anyone's way. Those with money looked at their accounts and shivered at how the balances had shriveled in value each succeeding month. Those who had little had less.

Before leaving the house, Eugenie looked at herself in the long mirror as usual, but this time she disapproved. Her clothes were no longer stylish, and she looked plain dowdy, she thought, partly because she had resisted the rising hemlines and partly because the fabrics of her dated apparel were weary. It wasn't just that. Her mother's face with lines creasing the forehead, the crisscrossed marks on her cheeks, and wispy, discolored hair falling over the brow looked back at her. "My, my. That's what seven decades will do," she grimaced.

No matter. She had to get to the bank to check on the day's rates and to make some transactions. The short walk took a long time these days and only proud, determined effort kept her upright and sprightly. Of course she would meet some of her former students on the street or in businesses along the way, and so she could hobble later, but not now – not Miss Fuller.

Miss Fuller lurched and caught herself by leaning onto a hitching post that had been left on the street for historic embellishment. A couple of cars speeding down the thoroughfare had backfired and continued chugging as acrid smoke spewed behind them. Her detest and fear of automobiles became more pronounced, and several others nearby appeared shaken, too. "Dratted cars making all that noise!" Dratted. She hadn't used that term in years. It was a common curse word back home in Illinois. "I must be getting crotchety. Yes." She recalled a conversation she had overheard at the drug store a day or so ago, and was immediately engulfed in heat and prickles. "My hearing isn't what it used to be, but that gossip was clear, and I hope I didn't let on." The woman was right, of course. She had noticed it herself. Words just eluded her sometimes, and she would use 'and-a, and-a' until the word or train of thought came back to her. And yes, she was walking like a dodderer. It was so difficult to take one step after the other and proceed with grace. "I can't walk very far without the legs just refusing to go on. There's a name for it, and right now it eludes me – so time for more and-a's," and she smiled at her own awkward situation. By this time, she had entered the dimly lit bank – thinking that it reflected the mood of most people waiting their turn for service.

She continued her thoughts. "Tomorrow, I'll see Dr. Wallace. Another two dollars. I am making the man wealthy. He's a great chiropractor, though, and keeps me going in good health." Noting that she was next in line, Miss Fuller pulled some envelopes containing checks out of her pocketbook and was ready to make deposits as the bank teller, a former student – now a middle-aged man with graying hair – greeted her respectfully as always.

A gentleman held the heavy door open for her as she exited the bank. "Why, Archie! Pray tell, what are you doing here during the school day?"

"It's my free period, Miss Fuller, so I'm doing an errand."

"Oh, my goodness! The policies are very lax, I see. That would never have happened during my day, and I wouldn't allow it now."

"It's good to see you again, Miss Fuller. You taught me well, and now I'm trying to follow in your footsteps. I really enjoy teaching math and physics, thanks to you." The amenities continued, but as he walked on into the bank, he felt like a young student who had just been chastised. He completed his errand and scurried back to school, even though he had an extra twenty minutes before his next class session.

By the time Miss Fuller returned home, the iceman had already made his rounds. "What a pity. If I'd been here, I'd have argued with myself about buying a 25-pound block. It seems like such a waste to have it melt so quickly in the icebox. Luther is always kind enough to give me a few loose chips from the truck. Since I wasn't here, I have no ice, and it's such a hot day. Oh, my! I'll go next door and ask for some. Just a bit of ice for an old lady? Eugenie, stop it." And she did stop talking, but she went next door and made her plea.

Such incidents were fodder for gossip that Miss Fuller was poverty-stricken. An oft-repeated story about her frugality – or perhaps eccentricity – was that she saw no need to have more than one light bulb for several lamps. She simply moved the bulb from lamp to lamp as she deemed necessary. Townspeople who were accustomed to borrowing money from her in order to preserve their financial reputations in the community knew better, but their lips were sealed, of course. Courthouse records, if anyone had chosen to check, would have shown vigorous financial dealings in real estate and businesses, including the long-standing Fuller Building on Main Street that was built shortly after she arrived in Riverside.

Looking into the future, probate records would indicate that properties and long lists of various stocks, many of which were connected to railroads and first purchased in Galesburg many years ago when the town was a primary railroad hub in America, Miss Fuller had no need to worry. Even at the height of the Great Depression, after losing a large part of her savings – just as others all around her – her assets still totaled more than a half million dollars, a remarkable feat at the time.

The Eugenie Fuller Building

The Eugenie Fuller Building, west side of Main and near Tenth
(erected circa 1887 and razed October 1937)
(3979-85-91 Main Street. 55 ft. on Main and 100 ft. deep)

The Fall
May 24, 1933

She knew she was going to fall and that there was no way she could catch herself. It happened. Eugenie landed with a thud on the large, braided rug that covered the center of the upstairs hallway. Only yesterday, a glimmered thought crossed her mind when she caught her shoe on the edge of the Heritage Oval and stumbled, but she had grabbed at the end table and only went down on one knee. She remembered that at the time, she had promised herself to move the rug.

Well, Genie, now you've done it. Gather your wits and get yourself up and back to bed. Nothing happened. She was flat on her stomach and couldn't turn over. She reached over and grasped the end table. It tilted and the vase with fresh flowers tilted more and crashed to the floor. Then the three-legged end table fell across her back, and water from the broken vase seeped onto her skin. She began to realize that her right leg had cramped and was causing a numbing pain. When she tried to lift her leg up, a charley horse, reaching from her hip area to the calf of her leg made her cry out. If she could just turn over. If she could just do a push-up and get some leverage so she could crawl into the bedroom and pull herself up by the side of the bed. Nothing worked and panic set in.

"Now, Genie, that's enough. Are you going to lie here on the floor practically naked until someone discovers you days from now in this same spot?" Who would come looking for her? No one. Only yesterday, she had told a friend that she was thinking of taking a train home to Galesburg. The word would get out that she was out of town. And here she lay. Immobilized.

She began to call out — first with pain and then to get attention from someone passing by. Time passed and she didn't know how much. The pain was excruciating, and she knew that at times she was screaming. Her voice sounded like a stranger's.

Young Sam Evans passed her house on his way home, next door. It was late, 10:30 or so, and he savored the adulations he had received at the Masonic Lodge recognition ceremony a few hours ago and marveled that he really had come home again if only for a visit. It was good to meet with his friends from high school days and remember nostalgic events. He stopped in the parlor to talk with his parents and Grandmama, then made his way upstairs. Suddenly he was very tired — so tired that he dropped across his bed by the open window. The slight breeze on this late May evening was soothing, and he promised himself that he'd lie there only a few minutes and then hang up his good clothes and go to bed.

He heard a moan. The moan changed to a wail. It must be a night owl, but it was unlike any he had ever heard. Then, "Help me, help me!" accompanied the wail, and he raised his head to look across to Miss Fuller's house — with her open window directly across from his.

"Miss Fuller! Oh, Miss Fuller!" There was no response except for pleas for help and sounds of mournful wailing. "Don't worry, Miss Fuller, I'll get help for you! Right away! Sam tore down the stairway and interrupted his parents who were still up, engaged in a serious conversation. Immediately, they all three went next door and tried to find entry. The front door was locked and probably bolted because the handy skeleton key, a common lifesaver in desperate conditions, didn't work. The front windows were secured tightly. Sam ran to the side door, then to the back, and then tried windows as he ran back to his parents.

"We'll have to call the Fire Department. The house is locked solid. She must have fallen. I wonder how long ago..." Only the upstairs windows were open and the desperate sounds wafted down from several of them.

It was midnight when the firemen placed a tall ladder against an upstairs open window, and one of them ascended and then another right after him. John Powell rushed downstairs to unbolt the front door while Casey, the head fireman, attended to Miss Fuller who was, by now, unconscious. He grabbed a sheet from the bed and covered her, knowing how mortified she would be to have townspeople report that she was found in an indisposed condition.

Two other firemen hurried upstairs with a stretcher, and the four men gently lifted her onto it and carefully carried her down the stairs to a waiting ambulance. She had regained consciousness and calming comments by the firemen were interspersed with tearful words of thankfulness for their arrival.

Through her harsh pain, she summoned Sam as the stretcher passed near him. "Thank you, Samuel. Thank you. You are a fine person – and a hero. Thank your family for me." People commented later as the news spread through town that even in a near comatose condition, she was ever Miss Fuller with impeccable manners.

Then she lost consciousness again and was not aware of being placed in the waiting ambulance and taken to the Riverside Community Hospital on Magnolia Avenue. In the Emergency Room, and later in Room 219, the work to save her life began.

Past Tense

It was May 28, 1933, when a nurse entered the small, white, chaste hospital room and roused Miss Fuller. It was time to check on her and to give her another shot of morphine to kill the pain in her lower back and right hip and to lessen the continuing mortification of the fire department finding her in an upstairs hallway of her home, practically naked, nearly comatose, and injured a few days ago. Nurse Jennie reached for her hand and held it gently. "Poor Miss Fuller, Dear Miss Fuller, how you have changed," she thought, and suddenly she was carried back to the memory of high school study halls where Miss Fuller's slightest glance as she gazed around the room while doing classroom checks caused each student to behave like one and focus on textbooks and writing assignments. Hearing the rustling skirts fade away was a time to relax, look around and know that she had been pleased with their demeanor, but no smirks or giggles were evident. She sometimes doubled back.

Now she lay helpless, her wispy, white hair, long faded from vibrant red, spread out over the pillow instead of the twist usually coiffed on top of her head. Her face was ashen, the creases deep, her voice that of an invalid who has lost the semblance of decision-making. Miss Fuller turned, pressed Jennie's hand in return, and queried, "Just a little bit of ice?" The beginning of a smile played around her face when her mouth closed around the small chunk that Jennie placed on her tongue. "How refreshing. How very refreshing," she said to Jennie as a way of thanks when the ice became slivers in her mouth. Nurse Jennie lifted the hypodermic needle, but Miss Fuller pushed it away. "No, not yet. I don't need it. I don't want it. I want to think. I want to go home. Does the doctor say I'm doing better?"

"I'm just the nurse, Miss Fuller, but you are sounding stronger to me today. I'll ask the doctor to stop by to see you. He was by earlier today, but you were asleep. He'll talk to you soon. My order is to give you the medicine, though, so if you don't take it, I'll need to write that on my chart."

"Write it. Just write it. I want to see Dr. Wallace. Write that down, too. Make sure it goes on my record. The hospital won't allow him in here because he's a chiropractor. He's been my physician for many years. Be sure to write that down." Jennie did, and prepared to leave the room. At the doorway, she turned and came back to squeeze Miss Fuller's hand again. And then she did something that at any other time in her life would have been brazen and unseemly. She leaned over and brushed her lips on Miss Fuller's forehead. Then she hurriedly left the room in case Miss Fuller had a comment. Miss Fuller did. "God bless you, Jennie, you are a lovely girl and just as sweet as the child I knew years ago – how many years ago? Twenty? More than that." She turned her head away from the window's light and the march back in time began again.

Was it possible that she was reviewing her life the way people were said to do as they were drowning or nearing death? Why were thoughts coming to her that had been dormant for so many years? Why was she suddenly feeling guilty about incidents or comments she'd made that had seemed perfectly appropriate and innocent when they first occurred. Why were they rushing back as if she could still make amends? Why was she feeling this huge boulder inside her that was bogging her down and causing her to want to scream? Why was she suddenly aware that she called out for Abe and for her dad and for her mom and sisters Emily and Charlotte? But especially for Abe. The calming thought came as it often did these days. "Genie, it's going to be all right. It's all right, Genie." His voice was always gentle, quieting, and she sometimes felt that a breeze had just brushed by her. One day she even felt tendrils of her hair moving gently across her forehead and needed to brush them away from her eye. So it wasn't her imagination.

She shifted her position and felt cards against her arm that had shifted along with her move. Cards and notes from well-wishers were there. She couldn't see to read them. What on earth had happened to her glasses? No, she couldn't see to read, but the nurses told her about the cards as they were delivered to the room. Most of them had been hand delivered to the hospital as soon as people heard the news. The news. How awful. How could she have been so slow to get to the bathroom? How could she have removed her clothing in the bathroom and then had to walk to the bedroom for more? How could she have tripped across the worn braided rug with the hole she had been reminding herself to mend? And why didn't she get up and put on a fresh gown and go back to bed? She knew the answer to that question – knew it for hours – until her cries for help were answered. And now here she was. And the gossip would be juicy. And she realized she no longer cared. Why was that? She'd had a lifetime of caring about what other people thought. Not that she didn't do as she pleased, but she still cared about what others thought. "What will people say? What will people think?" Those had been words to live by in her small Illinois community, so even when she rebelled, she cared.

Release from that firm admonition was wonderful. It must be the medication. Dr. Wallace had warned her. "If ever you have to see another doctor, be extremely cautious about taking medicines. Your body is not used to them and will react much more strongly than someone who is used to taking patent medicines or prescriptions. What would make an ordinary person feel better could be lethal for you." She had only half listened because that kind of situation would not occur. She was absolutely opposed to putting foreign substances into her body, and she would just negate that idea to anyone who proposed it. Did she hurt? Absolutely, but she would just put up with it. The doctors prescribed it anyway, and she was suspicious that when she was feeling woozy or had fewer aches than usual, the nurses had done their duty. Maybe there was room for compromise.

Miss Fuller nodded and was soon fully asleep when the shift change occurred. Jennie told her replacement that Miss Fuller was to be awakened when the doctor came by because she had some questions for him and had missed his morning round. Within the hour, the second shift nurse had checked on Miss Fuller who was still sleeping or at least groggy and had injected the prescribed morphine.

Eugenia left the schoolhouse and set out by herself on Fuller Road. The winding trail curved. While she was walking up the hill, she could not see past the curve, but she knew that home was just a short distance past it. It was the first time she had traveled the road by herself. Usually her sisters, neighbor kids, and sometimes the teacher or someone's parent would keep each other company. They would talk, sing songs or recite poems. Sometimes they sat down on the side of the road and ate the remainders of their lunches. Today, Eugenia noticed the quietness, the new leaves on trees, the scampering rabbits, the flitting birds, the huge cumulous clouds, and the quietness grew. Her shoes scrunched against the small rocks in the pathway, and slipped a bit on the green moss and grasses newly wet from the spring shower a few minutes ago. She felt immense happiness and contentment and not a shred of fear of walking home by herself. She even forgot why it was that she was traveling alone. Soon she would be home where the house was filled with love and acceptance.

When Doctor Wells walked into the room minutes later, prepared to pull the morphine medication, he found a nurse and emergency house doctor who had just pulled the sheet over Miss Fuller's head.

DEATH CERTIFICATE

RIVERSIDE COMMUNITY HOSPITAL

RIVERSIDE, CALIFORNIA

Name: Eugenie Fuller

Date: May 28, 1933   3:00 in the afternoon

Cause: shock following fracture of right hip and pelvis.
          Odema of lungs.

W. B. Wells, M.D.

Entry in the records:

Eugenie Fuller

A member since October 22, 1887.

Funeral (#414) June 1, 1933. Old Age

Minister: Reverend Daniel L. MacQuarrie

United Presbyterian Church
Magnolia Avenue,
Riverside (Arlington), Calif.

The Riverside Press

FINAL HONORS TO BE PAID MISS FULLER
May 30, 1933

Services will be conducted Thursday for Veteran Teacher

Funeral Services for Miss Eugenie Fuller, who passed away Sunday afternoon as the result of a fall in her home, will be held Thursday afternoon at 3 o'clock in the chapel of M. H. Simons & Co., it was learned today from C. L. McFarland, who has been in communication with the relatives of Miss Fuller in Galesburg, Ill., and is making arrangements for the funeral. Interment will be in Olivewood Cemetery.

Miss Fuller was well-known to many Riversiders by reason of her long connection with the city schools. She was Principal of the High School in the early nineties, during a period when many who have since become prominent in the nation's life were members of graduating classes.

Among those who studied under Miss Fuller were Dr. Ray Lyman Wilbur, President of Stanford University, who was Secretary of the Interior in President Hoover's Cabinet; Charles Sumner Dole, prominent in public life in Hawaii; Dr. Loye Holmes Miller, naturalist and later member of the faculty of the University of California; Miss Marcella Craft, internationally famous opera star; Edmund Heller, naturalist, who accompanied Colonel Theodore Roosevelt on his expedition into British East Africa in 1909; Theresa May Wilbur, for many years head of national Y.W.C.A. work; Dr. Walter M. Dickie, until recently State Director of Public Health; Ivan B. Rhodes, prominent in state and international Y.M.C.A. work; Harvey Hall, author of works on botany and member of the faculty of the University of California, and Cloyd Heck Marvin, former President of the University of Arizona and now President of George Washington University of Washington, D.C.

Miss Fuller Paid Final Tribute of Respect by Sorrowing Friends
June 1, 1933

Sorrowing friends, among them many who had been students in her classes in the High School during the formative years of the school system in Riverside, paid their last tribute of respect at funeral services for Miss Eugenie Fuller this afternoon.

These tributes took the form of a wealth of flowers that were banked about the casket, in the chapel of M. H. Simons & Co., where the rites were observed at 3 o'clock. The pallbearers were students of various classes that Miss Fuller taught... C. L. Reynolds, G. Ethelbert Dole, Emmett L. Singletary, Jules Covey, J. S. Kearne, and C. O. Perrine.

The services were simple, in keeping with the desires of Miss Fuller. Rev. D. L. MacQuarrie, pastor of Magnolia Avenue Presbyterian Church... preached the funeral sermon...

Interment: Olivewood Cemetery on Central Avenue, Crypt # 111, Riverside.

Olivewood Cemetery, Riverside, California
Entry number: 5949. Crypt: 111, second from bottom, 4th row. June 1, 1933.

In addition to her crypt in Riverside, Eugenia's family placed a marker at the Fuller Cemetery, on the family farm, near Galesburg, Illinois.

Everything Was Gone

Counsel C.L. McFarland, a longtime friend and legal consultant to Miss Fuller over the years, quickly notified Emily in Galesburg and kept in touch with her even though the administrator of the estate was J. E. McGregor. Eugenie owned several properties in town – building lots, houses, the Fuller Building on Main Street – and she had several interests in Galesburg plus her many stock holdings and other investments. The work was time consuming and would cover some time. Until other arrangements could be made, Mr. McFarland volunteered to make sure that her yard on Seventh Street was properly maintained – out of friendship and respect for Miss Fuller's desire to always keep the grounds meticulous. They both had hailed from Galesburg and his many contacts with friends back home made Judge McGregor's work easier with the coordination. Eventually, they arranged to have some favored furniture, artifacts, pictures, and books shipped to Emily and other relatives, but he personally wanted to examine the many books, manuscripts, correspondence, and miscellaneous papers and determine which ones were to be donated to the city museum, to the high school library, and to special designees mentioned in her Will. It would be more efficient to continue to house them on Seventh Street until the house cleared Probate.

A lengthy trial and other matters required his full attention, but he at last calendared time to honor Miss Fuller's desires, and his own, on behalf of the historical significance of her life's work in Riverside. He was aware that she had penned her autobiography and had written two novels. Novels, yes, but they contained sketches and events of life in Riverside. He had urged her to publish them, but she advised him that could happen only sometime after her death. "Unlike Mark Twain, I won't set a time limit," she laughingly told him. He was eager to read them and regretted having waited so long. Where had the time gone? He knew that he had to hurry to complete the moving of her records, study them and relegate them to the proper interested organizations.

He entered the house to stark emptiness. There were no books, no manuscripts, no journals, nothing. Everything was gone. Fear gripped him and heightened when he learned that the house had gone through probate and was about to be sold. The person Judge McGregor had authorized to oversee the property was quite pleased with his work and said that naturally it was necessary to dispose of the clutter within the house and carriage house, another storage area. "We gave what furniture that was left – like the fainting couch and some chairs – to some of the neighbors. The real chore was getting rid of the books and papers. There were stacks. She must have kept everything."

Contacts with Riversiders, Emily and other relatives who might have had copies of Eugenie's work were fruitless.

Everything was gone... except memories for the record.

Miss Fuller's authentic fainting couch. Her neighbors kept this couch in their basement for years. The Leonard Covel family secured it, refurbished it, and cherish it.

Epilogue

The information that follows gives you a picture of how former students of Eugenie Fuller and those who were involved in her life or studied about her in later years enjoyed reliving some of the memories from time gone by. Participants joined each other in two separate meetings hosted by the author and her husband, Leonard Covel, to celebrate the revival of Miss Fuller's inspirational life story. The first assembly was at Lable's Deli on Central Avenue and the second one was held at The Eugenia Fuller Education Center in the Brockton Arcade, next door to The Manhattan Grill, also owned by the Covel family.

The author, Janice Covel

Mr. and Mrs. Roy Haglund

Mr. Haglund, President of the Riverside Pioneer Historical Society
confers with Tom Patterson, Local Historian with
The Riverside Press-Enterprise

224

A presentation about Miss Fuller's life to the
Riverside Pioneer Historical Society in September 1977 led to further
research about her life in Galesburg, Illinois and Riverside, California.

Pioneer Historical Society of Riverside

OFFICERS

President   R.L.Haglund
Vice President Ed.M.Uhlig
Secretary   Mrs.A.G.Paul
Treasurer   Mrs.Howard G.Hall

Honorary Vice Presidents
Carl Helmick
Mrs.C.G.Scott

Executive Board Members

Term Ending 1978
Cleo E.Thomas
Mrs. James P.Warner

Term Ending 1979
James M.Wells
Mrs. Ernest S.Wilson
Mrs. Clarence Worsley

Term Ending 1980
Mrs. Delphin Difani
Mrs. Alvin J.Nielsen
Mrs. Edward P.Trausch

Ex Officio
Charles A.Hice
Warren Schweitzer
John Brumgardt

NOTICE OF MEETING

     The next meeting of the Pioneer Historical Society of Riverside will be held in the California Room of the Mission Inn on Sunday October 2,1977 at 12:30 P.M.
     The menu will be Baked Chicken and the cost will be $ 4.25 , including tax and tip.

PROGRAM

" EUGENIA FULLER AND THE ORIGINAL RIVERSIDE HIGH SCHOOL."

BY MRS. LEONARD R. (JAN.) COVEL.

     Mrs. Covel is Principal of Highland School and has done a considerable amount of research on the life and work of Miss Fuller,even to the extent of visiting her birthplace in Galesburg, Illinois this past summer .

     At this the beginning of a new school year it is most appropriate that we hear something about the pioneering days of the High School and the first woman principal . We hope that you will bring a guest , someone interested in education or possible someone who knew Miss Fuller or perhaps someone interested in coming again to the Mission Inn.

     Dues at $ 2.00 per person are now payable for the year 1978 and may be paid at this meeting.

     Mrs. Arthur Paul , our Secretary , is greatly improved in health but cannot assume this responsibility again but our Vice President will take reservations.

RESERVATIONS SHOULD BE MADE BY THURSDAY NOON SEPTEMBER 29th.

Please call Vice President Ed.Uhlig 684 - 3157 or President Haglund 683 - 5462

The author named her tutoring center in honor of Miss Fuller

An expression of gratitude to the many people
who contributed to this book, <u>For the Record</u>

```
                    The Eugenia Fuller Education Center
                            at Riverside
                          3749 Central Avenue
                      Riverside, California 92506
                              784-3749

                                            May 14, 1980


     You were so kind to me a short time ago when you shared your
     memories about Eugenie Fuller with me.  You'll be pleased to
     hear that I finished the dissertation in 1977, continued to
     research the life of Eugenie and now finally am about to
     plunge into writing the story of her life.

     As a side - and an important side - interest, I'm officially
     establishing a tutoring center in Miss Fuller's honor on
     May 25, 1980.

     You are cordially invited to a

          BRUNCH AT LABLE'S DELI

          3739 Central Avenue

          10:30-12:30, May 25, 1980.

     After brunch, we will move to 3749 Central (next door) and
     dedicate the Education Center.

     Please come.

               Sincerely,


     - - - - - - - - - - - - - - - - - - - - - - - - - - - - - - -

     Yes _____ I will attend the brunch in honor of Miss Fuller.

     Yes _____ I need transportation.  Please underline if you use
               a walker or wheel chair.

               My phone number is _____

     No _____  I am sorry that I cannot attend the brunch in honor
               of Miss Fuller.


                              _____
     (invitation includes     _____
     spouse or friend)              Name/Names
```

Dr. Edmund C. Jaeger

As a young college student, Mr. Jaeger often stopped to chat with Miss Fuller when he passed her house on 7th Street. He lived on 6th. Dr. Jaeger became well known for his extended works on desert ecology. He was Professor of Zoology for 30 years at Riverside City College and is the author of many books and articles. For a time, the author drove him to Redlands for Fortnightly meetings. He talked all the way about the palm trees and other vegetation we passed.

George Herrick, age 94 at the time this picture was taken. A resident of Riverside since 1889, and deeply indebted to Miss Fuller's influence.

John R. Jahn credited Miss Fuller for his lifelong love of mathematics. During the hours the author visited with him, he was often distracted by brokers and others contacting him with stock market options.

Author's Note

This manuscript has been pending for many years and that has been fortuitous in finding and verifying information. Sometimes I spent hours, days, weeks on a chapter and thought I had facts nailed down, only to discover new information that contradicted or at least varied from what I'd written. For instance, when I first traveled to Galesburg and visited the Fuller cemetery, I dutifully took pictures of Eugenia's markers and talked with the longtime groundskeeper who told me about the funeral service. Several months later, when I wanted to ascertain the date that her body was shipped back to Galesburg, my research led me to a crypt that houses her body in the Olivewood Cemetery in Riverside. If conferences with former students, townspeople and business associates had been limited after talking with only four or five, we would have a very narrow profile of a strict and lofty teacher and school administrator, instead of an energetic, fun loving woman who was said to be a crackerjack of a teacher, a sharp businesswoman, a loyal friend, and an intellectual who walked with students as easily as presidents of universities.

There were stretches when I could write vociferously and other stretches when words would come, but the real person was missing. It has been important to me to show her as a flesh and blood person rather than giving an account of statistics and formal records. I wanted to present personal material, especially since her manuscripts and journals were never given the light of day – although I keep searching every lead.

I made a commitment many years ago to write someone's story because her work was destroyed. I hope it related to Eugenia/Eugenie Fuller who through the years has become a role model for doing what's fair, right and substantial, and vowing that justice will prevail. With passion, I say to you that we both have lived believing that learning is a joy forever. Since you have read to this point, that surely must be true of you, too.

A Supplement

FOR THE RECORD

Selected clarifying, edifying, and verifying data of Miss Eugenia/Eugenie Fuller's life are available in Appendices A and B, followed by an annotated bibliography.

Riverside's Main Street, circa 1903
Eugenia Fuller Building in background

Appendix A

Notice that Eugenia's name is spelled with an ia or ie

Comments about Eugenie Fuller as Related by Former Students ascribed in Interviews and Written Records

"Miss Fuller was a crackerjack, a tremendous person. Very fair – not the type to throw them (the kids) on the floor and stomp on them – but Frances Stewart did, and P. S. Lord did the same. Miss Fuller built up the Riverside High School to an A-1 rating. Quite a mathematician herself. She was qualified and taught all the higher math and tried to get her students into the best schools. She worked it this way. To get into Berkeley, you had to have algebra and plane geometry. She put in advanced algebra and plane geometry 3rd year, and then everyone had to take her math the 4th year, and she made sure they did well.

They didn't have many parties. No dances – strong church town. No P.E. until about 1910. Miss Gandy did that on the side. You had the feeling that there were no discipline problems.

Ernest L. Ray was really a strange fellow. One day I made an error in using wherefore for therefore. He lectured me for about 5 minutes. I got sent out of the room and was sent to assembly and had to stay after school.

One girl who had been caught cheating on a test had to get up and publicly apologize in front of the whole student body. Miss Fuller saw to that.

Miss Fuller had a very commanding voice with quite an edge. Her voice carried well. She went to the Philippine Islands and had a couple students come over. She sponsored them – two high school boys – they had done a lesson for her, and she brought them here.

She was definitely a bachelor girl — not prim and proper as was common for the day. Lyman Evans and Holmes were Board members who supported Fuller." (Hill)

————

I was invited to the home of Mrs. Beverley Hargis whose mother, Mrs. Alice Chandler Baden, her three sisters and a brother-in-law were excited about helping me "put a puzzle together."

Miss Fuller dropped out of sight," said Cliff. "I remember seeing her only once after she retired. She came into the store." The four sisters in the interview agreed that contact was lost when she retired.

There was some disagreement about her age at retirement. One said, "Oh, yes, she was ready to retire." Another disagreed. The picture of Miss Fuller in the 1909 yearbook was examined. She looked fortyish. "But when we were young, that was old."

"But she was younger than Miss Van Slyck who thought she should have had Miss Fuller's job. There was bad feeling."

"Miss Van Slyck was jealous of Miss Fuller — was much stricter, too — to the point of almost being mean.

"And Miss Fuller was strict, too. And she could really put it to you in class. One time she asked me a question, and I stood and began my answer. I said, 'Well, it carries the thought that... and she said, 'How, Clifford? In a baby carriage?'"

"Oh, but when our schools separated and we got Mr. McWhinney (sic). What we did to that poor man! I was so naughty..."

"But you didn't get caught."

"Oh, sometimes I did — but not the time I threw a weeney on his chair and he sat on it. All the others saw me do it — and when he sat down, everyone laughed and he couldn't figure out why we were laughing."

"Near the end – though – there were problems…"

"Yes," said Cliff, "and I know what they were."

The women said, "You do?" almost in unison and then there was silence. The researcher alluded to a story she had heard about high school pregnancies.

And then everyone began to talk again.

"Yes, that was it. Two of the girls in particular had a lot of difficulty. One was M_____ W_____. She could tell you a lot." Her picture was pointed out.

"But someone has remarked that the older businessmen rather than the high school boys were involved," the researcher commented.

"Oh," sniffed one. "There was plenty of shrubbery to hide behind. A lot of it was going on with the high school boys." (Chandler-Baden, three sisters, and a brother-in-law)

———

"Miss Fuller was a thrifty person. One thing I remember. She had pretty good discipline. We used to meet on the third floor. She loaned money. My mother borrowed money from her at 12 per cent. We never knew much about her. She was quite a plump woman – not too tall. She was pretty well liked by the students. She died in a room. I don't know if I should say that. I always liked her. She was a wonderful algebra teacher. She was good. I was not too good in algebra.

"She dressed rather plainly. Skirts and blouses were very common. Miss Van Slyck wanted the job that Miss Fuller had. I can remember she was very sedate and tall and much older than Miss Fuller. She was real tall and a good teacher. I had her for English. She was the sister of Judge Noyes. The 3rd floor was where we studied. We didn't have many athletics. We'd open the windows and go to them and exercise. The aristocratic and high-toned people lived by the orange groves. Their kids came to school by streetcar.

"When the high schools were separated, the boys had a terrible time. The Osborne boy went through the window and he was always lame after that. Some of the elementary schools had terrible discipline. Some of the sixth graders, especially. I never saw Miss Fuller after I was out of high school, although I worked at the light company for years. Mr. Wheelock taught history in high school, I think.

"Miss Fuller was very businesslike. The very distinguished people came out of the high school. The Hyatt Girl, Wilbur, who became President of Stanford. The Willburs were all smart people." (Stinchfield)

————

"Miss Fuller taught me trig. She told me over and over I should go into math. I told her I decided to be an electrical engineer. She was stern in some respects, but she had good discipline ability and was exceedingly friendly. She held the line very firmly – even with teachers. Even Mrs. ___. Someone confided to me that Mr. ____ smoked a pipe downtown, but he never smoked at school. Miss Fuller didn't permit smoking.

"Miss Fuller pled with Merle to practice with me. She gave me a topic – Lincoln as a Soldier. I had to give a five-minute speech. But Merle didn't help me with that. I really didn't want to do it. Merle and I had made radio receiving equipment so that we could talk across town. In those days, I lived near Highgrove and didn't have electricity, so Louis Carmen and I had to give the salutatorian address and we gave it on the radio and we had the equipment rigged up.

"Clyde Hecht was the cheerleader for the school. He was a great favorite of Miss Fuller's. He cheered for the debating team. He was very outgoing. He later became President of George Washington University.

"I met Miss Fuller once on the street about 2:00 one afternoon – somewhere around 1930. At that time, I was teaching math and physics at the high school and college. She said, 'Hey, how come you're down here. I never let _my_ teachers go downtown during school hours." (Twogood)

————

"Miss Fuller was Principal when I graduated from high school, and I remember her well. But I remember her as older than this picture. She was the executive type and a very positive person. I was really kind of scared of her. She was friendly in her way, but she was pompous in her way. There was a wild party up on the mountain and, if I'm not mistaken, Miss Fuller was there. There were some bad acts and the story spread. Jo Nielsen and Jennie Ennis may have been there. The citizenry got upset and so we were separated. There was a big assembly hall in the new girls' high school. We kept our books in the desks. Every other row in the high school was for boys and girls. A year of the girls and boys in rows. Then Poly was built. It didn't do much good. We stuck notes in the boys' desks and couldn't wait to get to school. A. N. Wheelock, the Superintendent – his office was right across the office from the high school principal.

"I wanted so much to go to college. My father couldn't spare me. We had put in a business course during my senior year, so if I ever had to, I could make a living. It shut me out of taking botany and naturalist courses. I went back the 5th year and they needed someone in the principal's office. I worked for Mr. Winne. He was altogether different. A quiet man and soft spoken. He didn't have too much personality to tell you the truth. This was very noticeable after being with Miss Fuller who was so forceful and positive.

"I came in (to school) on a streetcar from Arlington. The big boys would scare the daylights out of you. One of the streetcars was green and had velvet furnishings. The boys would get in back and move it up and down – right by the canal – but nothing ever happened. Back there in those days, a French family lived in the country, and they had the cutest little Shetland pony and a little surrey. He brought his daughter to school in it.

"Miss Fuller had good order in school, but she was lenient in spots. Whinney (nickname) was dull by comparison. I have it in my mind that Miss Fuller was supposed to be chaperone at the time of that party. Regarding the stories about the Wheelock and Fuller animosity, I can believe it. I can see them. Mr. Wheelock's office was right across from the Principal's (Miss Fuller's)." (Babcock)

———

It was late fall when Marie Goethals Leibert returned from two years of college work in Belgium. "I had expected to have to wait until the following September before enrolling at U. S. Berkeley (sic UC). Just before Christmas, I met Eugenie Fuller, the Principal of the High School, on Main Street. She asked concerning my plans, then suggested that I enroll for the Spring term which would begin about the middle of January. She would send my transcript that day and write Benjamin Ide Wheeler, the President, at the same time. All would be settled except housing... Two phone calls and Berkeley was ready for me. I bought a ticket and left San Pedro at 4 p.m. one evening, and the ship arrived in San Francisco at 8 next morning..."

"Yes, there were all kinds of stories about her discipline at the end, but it was positively not her fault. A number of girls got pregnant and their parents took them into Los Angeles to have abortions. It wasn't because of Miss Fuller. What happened was that the new cars were bought by men with jobs, and they'd invite the high school girls to spend a day with them – take them on trips, and the girls got pregnant. Not one of those pregnancies came from the high school boys." (Leibert)

––––––––

"She didn't care for me much and I didn't care for her. She didn't like me with good cause. She made me get up in front of the whole school, two or three hundred people, and apologize for being a bad girl. It was done in an assembly between classes. She used to put E. F. on the back of notes for tardiness and absences so teachers would accept students into class. I could make an E. F. as well as she and my line was as long as hers for forged excuses or being absent. We had real arguments. She would just spit out her words, but didn't raise her voice.

"I had to have her okay (on an application) to go to college. She said she'd have to think about it and to come back tomorrow. I had to go back three or four times – and finally Mr. Wheelock said that if she told me that again, I should come to him and he'd write the comments.

"I went to high school from 1904-1908 and then to Stanford and when I made Pi Phi, that nearly killed her. 'I hear you're a Pi Phi!' Oh, she was mad. She was also Pi Beta Phi." (Reynolds)

"Eugenia Fuller was Principal of The High School when I attended and graduated in 1910. She really was a character. Some of us were more or less afraid of her. She seemed fond of Edmund who later became my husband. In school, she seemed to approve of whatever he chose to do, things no one else could do." (Irene R. Allatt)

"I was very fond of her. I had her in high school, too. She was a wonderful teacher and principal. A brilliant woman. She wanted to be generous, but couldn't quite be. Yet she put boys through college, and she traveled around the world over the years. Once she brought home quite a pile of Panama hats.

"Mrs. Atwood had a government position and visited all the Indian tribes and was very close to the Indians of the Yellowstone National Park. She was made a member of that tribe and was a friend of the chief. Miss Fuller was chairman of Indian Affairs Committee for the National Woman's Club. They often disagreed.

"Mr. Strang, a Board member, was a crotchety old man. His home was on Seventh Street. He was difficult to get along with.

"She had a beautiful opal ring. It meant so much to her.

"We had some boys of prominent families and she disciplined them and they decided to get her. They were spoiled and unruly.

"I had things my way with Mr. Wheelock. I got my credentials and was a teacher at Bryant and then principal at Lowell School." (Johnson)

Comments made at a 1909-1910 Riverside High School reunion at Chauncey's Restaurant on June 26, 1976:

"Oh, my yes, Miss Fuller, I remember well. When she entered the room, she commanded respect. I only wish she were here to handle some of these young people. She wouldn't permit what goes on now." (Hill)

———————

"Each morning we had assemblies. Not very long. Just a few minutes. She was in charge. Then we went to our classes. She was a dominant person." (Hagen)

———————

"She taught classes – algebra, geometry, trigonometry. She was demanding in her expectations. She really liked to teach the boys. Wanted them all to be engineers." (Sullivan)

———————

"She favored the boys. But if she got down on you – like Archie (Twogood), she didn't let up. She would get down on students. She tried first to get boys into engineering. Architecture and law were good, too. Her students entered easily in Stanford and Berkeley and got high jobs." (Carmen)

———————

The following excerpts were taken from the Sibyl of 1909. The Sibyl is the High School Yearbook. Just for Fun section, page 53, had laughable quotes of the year:

Miss Fuller, finding Howard Fletcher asleep in algebra class: "Oh, well, we won't wake him up. He isn't bothering anybody, anyway."

Fletcher was mentioned in quips of 1910:
Mr. North: "Well, I suppose you have all mastered your lesson for today."
Howard Fletcher: "Yes, what is it?"

An unedited testimonial to Miss Fuller by an alumnus in a follow-up correspondence after the 1953 reunion:

Miss Fuller came from Galesburg, Illinois, in the late 1880's to teach in the Arlington School on Palm Avenue. I was her pupil there during my 7th and 8th grades. She transferred to the High School in the Fall of 1890 at the same time that I did, so I had the advantage of six years of her guidance. In arithmetic she taught me methods of analyzing a problem that have served me to this day (and are being passed on to my granddaughter).

She gave simple instruction in Biology and Human Anatomy during which she dissected a coyote for us. She assisted me after I had made many clumsy efforts, by teaching me how to make a bird skin for scientific collection, how to draw a specimen accurately. She taught me correct grammatical structure in writing and speaking English. She was a born teacher with a craftsman's pride in her work.

I owe her more than I do any other teacher for she took a personal interest in my going to college – as she did many of her boys. She never forgot one of us.

Written by **Loye Miller,** March 25, 1954. Dr. Miller was a world-renowned ornithologist and Professor of Biology and Zoology at UCLA and UC Berkeley.

A sample cover page of the Sibyl, 1911

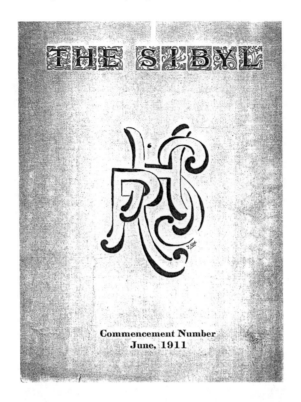

In Sibyl's Last Will and Testament, 1909:

Lastly, to our principal, Miss Fuller, who has watched and guarded us from the days of our freshmanship through the last days of senior maturity, we do leave our love and gratitude.

Looking Back

I interviewed Harv Smith in North Henderson, Illinois on 8/13/78. He was 87 years old and a native of the immediate area of Fullers. He was loquacious and made the following comments:

"Yes, I knew The Fullers. Samuel – He was a very prominent farmer and as I remember he was a quite fine horseman. We used to go by their place on our way to visit another family, and he had fine, beautiful horses.

"The girls kept the furniture that they cherished in the two side rooms in the back when they rented the farm.

"I had a cousin who rented it. William Rose rented it.

"I hung paper and I did some decorating there. I papered the house for them. The house was well-built and very special in its day. The woodwork was all walnut.

"The old barn had a basement. Imagine a basement in the barn. Mr. Fuller had a lot of fine cattle – and at night and when it rained or the weather got cold, he put them into the basement.

"When I saw Emily, she was at the Koonses. She was older. I was a kid and – I just happened to be there with the Koons boys.

"They were old – not heavy – good height and not fat – I don't remember much about them.

"I know they didn't go to a Henderson Church (two of them) and they didn't – couldn't go to the Swedes' Church because they couldn't have understood any of it.

"They may have gone to Greenleaf School. It was older than Mt. Joy and was two miles further down the road.

"Old Grandma Humes lived west of Mt. Joy – and when people talked about what to name the school, she said it's so high up, you should call it Joy on the Mountain."

(Anything you remember about their dress?) "No, they always looked nice, though. I always expected they were quite strict in their views.

"Blue cemetery was named for the Blue family. Eleanor Blue – was one of the finest women in the country. I never knew her but my parents talked a lot about her.

"Another thing. A woman jumped in the creek and drowned herself – water got high there every year. I fished there years ago – but no more. It was a rushing brook with some still places. (Tell me more abut her.) I don't know who the woman was but she had gone mad."

Additional comments were unrelated to the Fuller family and do not appear here.

Appendix B

Information that may clarify and support the manuscript

Census information for 1850, 1860, 1870.

Township 11 N 2 6. 1850 Census

(# of dwellings visited?) 1369.   (# of families visited?) 1415

Samuel Fuller	29	Farmer	Ohio
Lucinda	25		Illinois
Charlotte	2		Illinois

June 1, 1860 Census, Henderson Township, County of Knox, Illinois dwellings: # of visitations, 1515. Families: # of visitations, 1515.

(name)		(age)	(gender)	(profession)	(birth)
Samuel Fuller		37	M	farmer	Indiana
Lucinda	"	34	F		Illinois
Charlotte	"	12	F		Pennsylvania
Emily	"	9	F		Indiana
Eugenia	"	6	F		Illinois

Value of Real Estate, 2000 Value of Personal Estate, 600
attended school this year: Ch, Em, Eu

Page 13 of Township Henderson, Knox County shows the following information for the 1870 Census:

# of houses visited, 89. # of families visited, 89.

(name)	(age)	(sex)	(color)	(occupation)	(birth)
Fuller, Samuel	40	M	W	Farmer	Ohio
Jane	40	F	W	keeping house	Ohio
Charlotte	20	F	W	teaching school	Illinois
Emily	18	F	W	at home	Illinois
Jennie	16	F	W	at home	Illinois

Real Estate: 3200   Personal: 1320

No one in school during past year

There are many discrepancies in the information from the three census years. According to the 1870 census:
1870-16= 1854 – Eugenia's likely birthdate. If so, then Emily's birthdate would have been 1852 and Charlotte's in 1850.
Likely, the parents were married at 19 or 18.
However, the date of 1857 is the date listed on Eugenia's crypt in Olivewood Cemetery, Riverside, California. In 1933, The Press Enterprise gave her age as 76. Hence the birthdate of 1857.

Organization of PI BETA PHI FRATERNITY

Emma Brownlee and Fannie Whitenack were gathered in the latter's home, that the topic of fraternities was under discussion, which resulted in the founding eventually of Pi Beta Phi Fraternity.

"Why cannot we college girls also have a fraternity?" asked Emma Brownlee. The suggestion met with favor, and the five girls chose six other girls as co-founders of the proposed organization. On April 28,1867, a meeting was held in the Holt house, where Libbie Brook and Ada Bruen roomed, to organize the proposed sorosis. Ten of the eleven girls attended this meeting. Fannie Thompson was not present, though she had accepted the invitation to join the society. At this meeting Emma Brownlee was made temporary president and Nannie Black was made temporary secretary. A committee was appointed to draw up a constitution and nominate officers, and the grip was settled upon.

IN THE BEGINNING, The Pi Beta Phi Fraternity was founded under the name of I. C. Sorosis, on April 28, 1867, in Monmouth College, Monmouth, Illinois, by the following eleven students of that college: Nannie L. Black (Mrs. Robert Wallace), M. Libbie Brook (Mrs. John H. Gaddis), Clara Brownlee (Mrs. A. P. Hutchinson), Emma Brownlee (Mrs. J. C. Kilgore), Ada C. Bruen (Mrs. S. Graham), Maggie F. Campbell (Mrs. J. R. Hughes), Jennie Home (Mrs. Thomas B. Turnbull), M. Rosetta Moore, Ina B. Smith (Mrs. M. C. Soule), Fannie A. Thompson (died in 1868) and Fannie B. Whitenack (Mrs. Howard Libby). Jennie Nicol was the first initiate, and was regarded as one of the Founders.

(2) ILLINOIS BETA, LOMBARD UNIVERSITY, Galesburg, Illinois, was established June 22, 1872, by Mary Brook, as IOTA CHAPTER of I. C. Sorosis, with the following charter members: Sara A. Richardson, Carrie Brainard, Ellen McKay (Greenwood), **Charlotte Fuller (Risley)**, **Eugenie Fuller, Emily Fuller**, Emma Batchelder (Cox), Lucretia Hansen (Wertman), Genevieve Dart (Crossette), Elsie Warren and Clara Richardson (Putnam). At the Indianola Convention in 1886, the chapter became ILLINOIS BETA. Two hundred and seventy-one members have been initiated into this chapter, of whom twenty-one are deceased.

The founding of our Fraternity was not the outcome of a hasty, thoughtless school-girl's whim or sentimental flash, but the result of serious discussion and planning. The early days were teeming with sacrifice and service. The very name chosen by them, I. C., known to all Pi Phis, published their standard, and to the wisdom, intelligence and endurance of these women we owe the long and successful life of our Fraternity. To these pioneers, with their rare insight into the needs and demands of the rising generations of women for higher and broader intellectual and spiritual development and unity, all fraternity women of all creeds should offer homage.

Information from Google

A sample of real estate transactions from the Riverside County Recorder's Office

Index to Release of Mortgages 1901-1906 Book 3

		Parties Releasing	To Whom Given			BK - Page	
1901	4/13	Fuller, Eugene	Jarvis, Joseph	Apr 13, 1901	40- 20	40-20	Full
1901	1/18	Fuller, Eugenie	Sutton, Jno R.	Feb. 18, 1901	24-49	24-49	Full
1901	4	Fuller, Eugenie	Stephenson, Thos. B	June 1, 1901	33-288	33-288	Full
1901	2/13	Fuller, Eugenie	Grotzinger, Ferdinand	Jul 13, 1901	4-197	4-197	—
1901	6/7	Fuller, Eugenie	Whittier, Annie M.	Aug 26, 1901	21-121	15-233	Full
1902	4/14/23	Fuller, Eugenie	Thompson, Katie L.	Apr. 23, 1902	32-366	32-366	Full
1902	5/31	Fuller, Eugenie	Allinder, John W.	May 31, 1902	45-32	45-32	Full
1902	6/16	Fuller, Eugenie	Brown, George H.	Jun 16, 1902	21-173	21-173	Full
1902	14/9/8	Fuller, Eugenie	Ford, George	Sept 4, 1902	18-141	17-5	Full
1902	3/18/24	Fuller, Eugenie	Kemptner, E.D.	Nov. 22, 1902	21-72	16-302	Full
1903	29/6/11	Fuller, Eugenie	Jarvis, Joseph	Nov. 22, 1902	32-397	18-93	Full
1904	12/1/4	Fuller, Eugenie	Kemptner, E.O.	Dec 18, 1903	21-72	18-261	Full
1904	12/1/4	Fuller, Eugenie	Kemptner, E.D.	Dec 18, 1903	45-135	18-261	Full
1904	12/1/7	Fuller, Eugenie	Allinder, J. W.	Jan 7, 1904	37-161	37-161	Full
1904	14/3/10	Fuller, Eugenie	Dew, S. W.	Mar 10, 1904	32-164	32-164	Full
1904	35/3/29	Fuller, Eugenie	Grotzinger, Ferdinand	Mar 29, 1904	40-72	40-72	Full
1905	3/4/10	Fuller, Eugenie	Hurlbut, L. P.	Apr 10, 1905	58-130	45-111	Full
1905	15/5/6	Fuller, Eugenie	Strangham, S.C.	May 6, 1905	58-130	58-130	Full
1905	30 Nov 6	Fuller, Eugenie	Allison, J.L.	Nov 6, 1905	45-129	45-129	Full

Index to Notices of Action I 1893-1901

				Book	Page
1	Eugenie Fuller	Plaintiff	June 2, 1896	2	110
4 (org)	Eugenie Fuller	Plaintiff	Dec 18, 1897	3	27
38	Eugenie Fuller	Plaintiff 2	Feb 24, 1916	7	127

Before segregation of the sexes

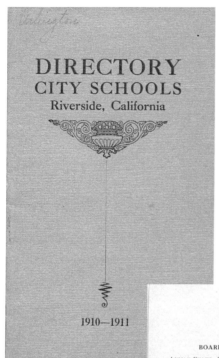

DIRECTORY
CITY SCHOOLS
Riverside, California

1910—1911

BOARD OF EDUCATION

LYMAN EVANS, President, Court House, Pacific 178; residence 454 Fourteenth St., Pacific 345.

MRS. H. A. ATWOOD, 904 W. Eleventh St; Pacific 188 J.

E. S. MOULTON, First National Bank, Pacific 108; residence 175 Magnolia Ave., Pacific 944 R3.

S. J. CASTLEMAN, First National Bank, Pacific 108; residence 29 Rubidoux Drive, Pacific 652.

W. G. IRVING, Evans Block, Pacific 718; residence Arlington Heights, Home 1928.

Regular meeting, second Tuesday each month

A. N. WHEELOCK, Superintendent City Schools and Clerk of the Board.
    Office: High School, Ninth St., Pacific 184. Home 1816.
    Office hours: School days, 4-5 p. m. Saturdays, 9-11 a. m.
    Residence, 1235 Lemon St., Pacific 1411 L.

RUTH P. JOHNSON, Superintendent's Clerk, residence 492 Kansas Ave., Pacific 1231 L.

2

HIGH SCHOOL, Ninth Street
Pacific 183; Home 1817

Eugenie Fuller, Principal, Hotel Reynolds, Pacific 54.

Mrs. F. G. N. Van Slyck, English, The Warrington, Pacific 557.

Mildred Averill, German, 468 W. Sixth St., Pacific 397 J.

Sarah J. Lee, Mathematics, 412 W. Tenth St., Pacific 583.

Della Gandy, Latin, English, 1489 Orange Grove Ave., Pacific 1330 R.

Elizabeth Cutting, History, 992 Walnut St., Pacific 1346 R.

Sophia N. Leal, Mathematics, 272 Bandini Ave., Home 1648.

Florence E Atkinson, English, 1431 Orange Grove Ave., Pacific 1327 J.

Ethel Wood, Modern Languages, 266 Lime St.

Harriet L. Southwick, Drawing, 266 Lime St.

E. A. Zumbro, Science, Chicago Ave., Pacific 852 R3

Ernest L. Rea, Latin, 907 Chestnut St., Home 1634.

Alfred M. North, History, 1459 Lemon St.

H. S. Upjohn, Mathematics, 1007 Fourth St., Pacific 1667 R.

Frederic W. Sanders, History, 170 W. Arlington Ave.

B. C. Benner, Modern Languages, 1489 Orange Grove Ave., Pacific 1330 R.

F. N. Featherstone, Athletic Director, 1035 Ninth St. Home 1081.

3

After segregation of the sexes

Directory
City Schools

Riverside, California
1911-1912

Girls' High School, Ninth Street
PACIFIC 163   HOME 1617

Eugenie Fuller, Principal, Hotel Reynolds, Pacific 54.

Mrs. F. G. N. Van Slyck, English, 451 W. 14th St., 1493 J.

Mildred Averill, German, 468 W. Sixth St., Pacific 397 J.

Sarah J. Lee, Mathematics, 412 W. Tenth St., Pacific 583.

Delia Gandy, Latin, 125 Lemon St., Pacific 1027 R.

Elizabeth Cutting, History, 992 Walnut St., Pacific 1346 R.

Florence E. Atkinson, English, 214 Prospect Ave., Pacific 1360 J.

Frederic W. Sanders, History, English, 170 W. Arlington Ave.

B. C. Benner, French, Spanish, 1489 Orange Grove Ave., Pacific 1330 R.

Harriet L. Southwick, Art, 1472 S. Lemon St., Home 3271.

G. R. Robertson, Science, 1223 W. Twelfth St., Pacific 100 J.

M. Alice Lamb, French, Spanish, 843 W. Third St., Pacific 1005 R.

Mrs. Emma A. Zinn, Stenography, Typewriting, 766 W. Twelfth St., Pacific 1075 J.

(4)

Boys' High School, North Street
TEMPORARILY LOCATED ON NINTH ST.

J. E. McKown, Principal, 814 Fourteenth St.

E. A. Zumbro, Agriculture, Chicago Ave., Pacific 852 R3.

Geo. W. Scott, Commerce, 360 W. Eleventh St.

C. C. Ockerman, English, 1448 Orange Grove Ave., Pacific 1099 R.

C. J. Wilcomb, French, German, 905 Lemon St., Home 1612.

A. M. North, History, 1459 Lemon St.

E. L. Rea, Latin, 907 Chestnut St., Home 1634.

Hugh Law, Manual Training, 386 Jurupa Ave.

H. S. Upjohn, Mathematics, 1007 W. Fourth St., Pacific 1067 R.

R. D. Wadsworth, Physiography, 160 Magnolia Ave., Pacific 944 J2.

A. H. Smith, Science, 1223 W. Twelfth St., Pacific 100 J.

M. S. Peckham, Spanish, 144 North St.

(5)

Graduates' Orations, Riverside High School, Class of 1905

In addition to Arthur Kaneko who had the highest honors, the following honor students in the 1905 graduation ceremony gave addresses, as quoted in The Riverside Press. (See pp. 134-136 for additional data.)

Holyday and Holiday
Miss Mattie Steele Singletary chose as her subject, "Holyday and Holiday," developing her thought in a very interesting way. She called attention to the fact that holidays have ever been prominent features of national life and sketched in succession clear-cut pictures of Thanksgiving, Washington's birthday, Fourth of July and Memorial day. Especially beautiful was her word picture of Memorial day in the cool, quiet cemetery on the hillside, and there followed a plea that the significance of this holyday, marking the nobler mood of the nation, be not forgotten.

A Word for Arbitration
"Arbitration" was the subject of a logical, well prepared oration by Charles Campbell. His remarks were pointed, and his delivery so good that his voice could easily be heard in all parts of the house. He rapidly sketched the growth of the idea of arbitration, from the time of early Greek history, and argued that as men have found that they can settle their differences by arbitration, so nations have begun to see that their differences can be ended in the same way. "The careful student of history," he said, "cannot fail to see in the future the realization of 'Peace on earth, good will to men.'"

The White Man's Burden
The next speaker was Miss Nellie Gleason, who handled her theme, "The White Man's Burden," in a wholly original and admirable manner. She presented an allegorical picture of the white man, burdened with a heavy load of the duties he owed to the less advanced races, climbing up the mountain (sic). Behind him plodded the brown man, the red man, the yellow man, the black man, following in his footsteps and looking to him for their advancement. Her thoughts were clear and well delivered and created a marked impression upon the audience.

Strenuous Mountain Trip

A pleasant innovation in commencement orations was Arthur Moulton's illustrated story of a trip he took up to the summit of Mount Shasta last summer, with a graphic description of all the attendant difficulties. A curtain was drawn across the stage and stereopticon views were shown picturing that interesting region and the successive stages of the climb.

The Poet She Loves

"There are few stronger desires in the heart of a romantic girl than to know the poet she loves," said Miss Mary Barclay in introducing her subject, "Ella Wheeler Wilcox." Then she followed with a very charming description of her meeting with this poet at Redlands a short time ago. She spoke of her personality and appearance, and sketched the history of her life in a sympathetic, interesting manner. To show the character of the woman, she quoted freely from her poems.

Conquest of the West

To Edgar Moon fell the honor of being the last speaker. His subject was the timely one, "What the Lewis and Clark Exposition Commemorates," and in developing it he emphasized the achievements of the heroes who added by peaceful conquest the great western region that is now so important and promising a part of the Union.

The music of the high school glee club added much to the interest of the program, and at each appearance the singers received an encore.

Diplomas Presented

Prof. A. N. Wheelock, superintendent of the city schools, awarded the diplomas. Accompanying the presentation of the prized parchment rolls he congratulated the members of the class of 1905 upon the successful completion of their high school work and spoke of the aspirations that should guide their lives in the future. These diplomas, he said to the class, (continued on Page 8 *which cannot be located*).

Annotated Bibliography

Galesburg, Illinois Sources

Calkins, Ernest Elmo. They Broke the Prairie. New York: Charles Scribner's Sons, 1937.

Catalogue of the Officers and Students of Lombard University, Galesburg, Illinois for the year ending June 20, 1877. Galesburg, IL, Galesburg Printing Company, 1877.

Hansen, Dorothy S. GALE' S "BURG" – The Mesopotamia of the West. Made available to the public by the Oliver Wendell Holmes Federated Woman's Club of Galesburg as part of their sesquicentennial observance.

Litvin, Martin. Hiram Revels in Illinois. Galesburg, IL: Log City Books, 1974.

Piatt, Roy Livingston. History of the Galesburg High School. Compiled and published by the author. (The Evening Mail Press) Galesburg, Illinois, 1899. (also on Google under the author's name)

Pooley, William Vipond. The Settlement of Illinois from 1830 to 1850. A thesis submitted for the Degree of Doctor of Philosophy, University of Wisconsin, 1905.

Record of the Centenary of Knox College and Galesburg. Galesburg, IL: Knox College, 1938. (Wagoner Printing Company, 1938).

Steele, W. L. Galesburg Public Schools: Their History and Work. 1861-1911. Galesburg, IL: Board of Education, 1911.

Swanson, James A. A History of Lombard College: 1851-1930. Western Illinois State College, Macomb, Illinois. March, 1955.

Webster, Martha Farnham. Seventy-Five Significant Years. The Story of Knox College. 1837-1912. Galesburg: Wagoner Printing Company, 1912.

Welge, Richard C. <u>Remnants of the Nineteenth Century Landscape</u> - <u>Knox County, Illinois</u>. Published by Knox County Historical Sites, Inc., Knoxville, IL. Printed by Wagoner Printing Co., Galesburg, Illinois, 1979. 96 pages.

Issues of the Times

Blum, Stella. <u>Victorian Fashions and Costumes from Harper's Bazaar, 1867-1898</u>.

<u>Godey's Lady's Book</u>. A magazine published from 1830-1878 for discriminating women who enjoyed articles by American authors, poetry and engravings.

Gullett, Gayle. <u>Becoming Citizens</u>. The Emergence and Development of the California Women's Movement, 1880-1911. Chicago: University of Illinois Press, 2000.

<u>Historic Galesburg</u>. 6 forty-five minute walking tours. Prepared by City Planning Dept., Galesburg, Ill. supported by a grant from the National Endowment for the Arts in Washington, D.C. No date.

<u>Our Home Monthly</u>. A periodical mailed to constituents. Philadelphia, PA. Some 1873 and 1874 issues.

Secretary of State Election Papers, 1911 Special Election. Cattell, H. G. (Argument for Women's Suffrage).

Secretary of State Election Papers, 1911 Special Election. Sanford, J. B. (Argument against Women's Suffrage).

Secretary of State Election Results, October 1911. Male voters passed by small margin on Oct. 10, 1911. 246,487 votes total cast in election. Suffrage passed by 3,587, less than 2%. Twenty-three issues on ballot. More voted on woman suffrage (yea, nay) than any other issue.

Stalcup, Brenda, Ed. <u>Women's Suffrage</u>. San Diego, CA: Greenhaven Press, Inc.,2000.

Interviews

Caretaker of the Fuller Family Cemetery, IL
Librarians at Galesburg Public Library
Librarians at Riverside Public Library
E-mails back and forth with volunteer railroaders
Secretaries at the Magnolia Presbyterian Church
Roy and Mrs. Haglund, President of Pioneer Historical Society, Riverside, CA
Elizabeth B. McKee, PEO home, 415 Main St., Knoxville, IL 61448
Tom Patterson, The Riverside Press Enterprise
Harv Smith, 87 years old and a long ago neighbor of the Fuller family in
    North Henderson, IL
Virginia Smith, Galesburg. Donated group picture at Fuller homestead
Mr. and Mrs. George Venn, Galesburg
Frank A. Ward, Galesburg attorney, President of Galesburg Historical
    Society (219 Weinberg Arcade, Galesburg, Ill 61401), Vice President of
    Illinois State Historical Society at the time of the interviews

Former students or residents who knew Miss Fuller in Riverside
Irene R. Allatt
Frances Allen
Gladys and Mr. Babcock
Alice Chandler Baden
Mr. and Mrs. Carmen
Esther Chamberlin
Emily Dole (went to Arlington School for a year plus 4 years in high school)
Mrs. Hagen
Carl Hambourg
Ethel Handcock Harp – wrote a cinquain for me. She learned the style from
    Miss Fuller.
May Henry – owned the house where Eugenie once boarded
George Herrich
Ruth Hill
John Royal Jahn – taught me about sun dials in our backyard – and the
    math involved.
Ruth Johnson
Marie Goethals Leibert

Edna Lockhart
Fred McEuen
M.B. Madden
Mrs. Miller
Mrs. Moffat
Mary Dunlap Scott
Mrs. Reynolds
E. L. Singletary
Myrtle Stinchfield (93 at the time)
Mr. and Mrs. Sullivan
Reba Thompson
Carolyn Thorsen
Archie and Dorothy Twogood
Dudley and Mrs. Wheelock
Julia Cornwall Wood
Some names withheld by request
Many more contacts without interviews. My thanks to those who sent articles and pictures, such as the 1902 graduation and Ina Blake Hampson's photograph.

Related Sources

Button H, Warren. "Creating More Useable Pasts: History in the Study of Education." State University of New York at Buffalo, 1978 AERA Annual Meeting, Division F, State-of-the-Art Address.

California State Railroad Museum, Front Street, Old Sacramento, CA. Librarians graciously devoted time and effort in searching records of the routes and conditions in the 1880s.

Fuller, William Hyslop. Genealogy of Some Descendants of Thomas Fuller. Volume IV and Supplements to I, II, III. Printed for the Compiler, 1919.

Galesburg Chamber of Commerce. 54 S. Kellogg Street.

Galesburg Historical Society. 325 N. Kellogg, Galesburg, IL 61402-1757.

Galesburg Public Library. 40 East Simmons Street, Galesburg, IL 61401-4597 (309) 343-6118.

History of Knox County, Illinois, 1878 (Mary Allen West information)

Illinois State Archives, Margaret Cross Norton Bldg., Capital Complex, Springfield. (217) 782-4682.
Illinois State Historical Records.

Knox College Archives, Knox College, Galesburg. Lombard Classes, 1867-1889, Box 16.

Lombard College records. Contact Registrar of Knox College. Box 16.

Mayer, Edward and Rose Fry (compiled by). Brief History of the Santa Fe Railway Lines in Southern California. Sunday, August 7, 1949. In 1886 a line known as the River, Santa Ana and Los Angeles, had constructed south from Highgrove, on the original main line. This was operated by California Southern.

Mayflower Descendants. Volume VII, 1905. Reference Dr. Samuel Fuller and Edward Fuller.

Poling-Kempes, Lesley. The Harvey Girls: Women Who Opened the West. Marlowe & Co., New York, 1991.

The Press-Enterprise. 3450 14th Street, Riverside, CA (microfiche)

Railway, Santa Fe Route. 4th Edition. Rand, McNally and Co., Engravers and Printers, 1892.

Riverside City Directory, 1905. Page 114. Fuller, Eugenie, Prin. High School, Res 1153 Main (note: house south of Elks' Club, S. E. Cor. 11 & Main [U.C. Bank now]. J. M. Wells.

Riverside Daily Press. "Fortieth Anniversary of Founding is Celebrated at Magnolia Church." Saturday Evening, November 8, 1919. Includes 3rd Endeavor Society founding in U. S. guided by Eugenie Fuller. (Young

People's Society of Christian Endeavour, a nondenominational evangelical society founded in1881 by Francis E. Clark, Portland, Maine.)

Riverside Public Records (Courthouse, Board Minutes, museum materials).

Riverside School Directories (giving dates of appointments, addresses, class assignments).

Riverside Historical Society. P. O. Box 246, Riverside, CA 92502. (Pioneer Historical Society preceded current name.)

Travelers' Official Railway Guide. August and October, 1886. National Railway Publication Company, 46 Bond St., New York City. Librarians at the California State Railroad Museum, after searching records extensively, estimated that a person traveling from Galesburg, Illinois to Riverside, California likely would have traveled the CBQ (Chicago, Burlington and Quincy) from Galesburg to Chicago and transferred to the Santa Fe to Los Angeles and then would have taken the California Southern to Colton or Riverside Highgrove Station. A stagecoach would have taken the person from Colton to Riverside. Buggies also were used for transportation.

Tyack, David B. (Ed.). Turning Points in American Educational History. Waltham, Mass.: Blaisdell Publishing Co., 1967.

Wikipedia. The Countess de Teba, as Eugenia/Eugenie was known before her marriage, wed Emperor Napoleon III on January 30, 1853. Educated and very intelligent, she acted as Regent during his absences. This is the most logical reason for the variances in Miss Fuller's name.

Riverside, California Sources

Avery, Lewis B., **Eugenie Fuller**, N. A. Richardson, W. H. Housh. "What Latitude Should Be Allowed High School Pupils in Election of Studies?" Overland monthly and Out West magazine. San Francisco. Volume 27, Issue 161, May 1896. pp. 553-556. http://name.umdl.umich.edu/ahj1472.2-27.161 Contact umdl-info@umich.edu for more information.

Blue and Gold. Pamphlet published by Longfellow School, Riverside, California, 1919. Printed by Polytechnic High School, Riverside. Valuable for its many ads of local businesses in the community. Verification of names of newspapers: Riverside Daily Press and The Riverside Enterprise for archive information.

Brown, John and James Boyd. History of San Bernardino and Riverside Counties. Volumes 1, 2, 3. Published by The Western Historical Assn, 1922. California Department of Public Instruction (Official Organ). Pacific Educational Journal, Volumes 1-2. "The Teachers' Institute Report," Pages 250-251, written by Edward Hyatt, Secretary for San Diego County. 1887.

California Teachers Association – www.cta.org/About-CTA/Who-We.../The-History-Of-CTA.aspx
        Founded in 1863 during the Civil War as the California Educational Society, CTA won its first major legislative victory in 1866 with a law providing free public schools to California children. A year later, public funding was secured for schools that educated nonwhite students. More early victories established bans on using public school funding for sectarian religious purposes (1878-79); free textbooks for all students in grades 1-8 (1911); the first teacher tenure and due process law (1912); and a statewide pension, the California State Teachers' Retirement System (1913).

Covel, Janice. Analysis of School Administrators' Careers in Riverside County from 1870-71 – 1974-75. Doctoral Dissertation, University of California, Riverside, 1977.

Covel, Janice. "Eugenia Fuller and the Original Riverside High School," presentation to Pioneer Historical Society of Riverside, California Room of the Mission Inn, Sunday, October 2, 1977.

Covel, Janice. "Eugenia Fuller: Influence on Educational Development and the Institutionalization of the Secondary Principal's Position, 1877-1912." Presentation at the Annual Meeting of California Educational Research Association, Bahia Hotel, San Diego, California, November 15-16, 1979.

Covel, Janice. "Thumbnail Sketch of Eugenia Fuller." Not dated.

Covel, Janice. Main Street Scene Puzzle, circa 1903, for Riverside's Centennial Celebration. Some puzzles available.

Holmes, E. W., Wm. A. Correll, Lyman Evans. Circular of Information of THE HIGH SCHOOL of the City of Riverside, California for the school year ending June 12, 1896. Walters & Crane, Printers, Riverside, California. Contains history of the high school, rules and policies, staff information, the three branches of study (Latin, Scientific and Commercial) and required classes for each for the four years of the programs.

Johnson, Wm. A., J. R. Jahn, Chas. E. Johnson, G. Ethelbert Dole, Marion Clark Mill, Stanley Richardson, Minnie Gaston, E. L. Covey, Frances Barber Fogleman. GOLDEN ANNIVERSARY RIVERSIDE HIGH SCHOOL ALUMNI REUNION. June 30, 1953.

Johnson, William A. Through the Years with William A. Johnson. A Family Album Assembled in 1955. Contains Miss Fuller's picture with community group.

Johnson, Wm. A. RIVERSIDE HIGH SCHOOL ALUMNI NEWS. Classes of 1906 and Prior Years. Fourth and Final Edition. May 20, 1954.

Klotz. Esther. Riverside and the Day the Bank Broke. Riverside, CA: Rubidoux Press, 1972.

Mayer, Edward and Rose Fry (compiled by). Brief History of the Santa Fe Railway Lines in Southern California. Sunday, August 7, 1949. (In 1886, a line known as the River, Santa Ana and Los Angeles, had been constructed south from Highgrove, on the original main line. This was operated by California Southern.)

Miller, Mrs. H. C., Chairman. MEMORY BOOK, Fiftieth Anniversary Homecoming. Class of 1924. Girls and Polytechnic High Schools, Riverside, California. June 14, 15, 16, 1974. History of high schools in Riverside and testimonials for Eugenie Fuller are in the latter part of the unnumbered manuscript.

Ne Plus. <u>Hitting the High Spots: A Rhythmical Relation of the Career of Arthur Newhall Wheelock</u>. Polytechnic High School Print Shop, Riverside California. no date.

Patterson, Tom. "A LADY OF PROPRIETY: Miss Eugenia Fuller Best Remembered of Teachers." Press Enterprise, Riverside, California, July 14, 1954.

Patterson, Tom. <u>A Colony for California</u>. Riverside, CA: Press-Enterprise Company, 1971.

Patterson Tom. "The mysterious firing of the inspirational Eugenia Fuller." Riverside Press-Enterprise, Riverside, California, October 30, 1977.

Patterson, Tom. <u>Landmarks of Riverside</u>. PRESS-ENTERPRISE CO., 1964.

Riverside City Schools. Directories (of staff), beginning 1908, Riverside, CA.

Riverside County Schools. Directories (of staff), beginning 1914, Riverside, California.

Riverside Title Company, <u>The Story of Riverside County</u>. Riverside, CA, 1957.

Rolle, Andrew F. and John S. Gaines. <u>The Golden State</u>. A History of California. Arlington Heights, IL: Harlan Davidson, Inc., 1979.

<u>Sibyl</u>. Periodical developed by high school students under the direction of English teacher, Mrs. F. G. N. Van Slyck, Riverside High School in the early 1900s. (Sibyl refers to a Greek prophetess.)

Southern California Panama Expositions Commission. <u>A History of Southern California</u>. Originally published 1914. Fresno, CA: Reprinted by California History Books.

<u>Spotlight, The</u>. <u>High School Newspaper</u>, Vol. 2, No. 14, Riverside, California, Jan. 12, 1922. Price: 5 cents

The Sibyl Alumni Edition, Riverside High School, Riverside, California, June, 1911. Gives information about all 674 graduates from 1890 through 1911.

White, John H. Jr. The American Railroad Passenger Car. Part 1. The Johns Hopkins University Press, Baltimore and London, 1978. ISBN 0-8018-2743-4, 0-8018-2722-1, 08018-2747-7

**Family Reunion Group Picture at the Fuller Homestead. Undated.
Courtesy Virginia Smith, Galesburg, Illinois**